D1566266

Palgrave Studies in Risk, Crime and Society

Series Editors
Kieran McCartan
Department of Health & Social Science
University of the West of England
Bristol, UK

Philip N. S. Rumney
Frenchay Campus
University of the West of England
Bristol, UK

Risk is a major contemporary issue which has widespread implications for theory, policy, governance, public protection, professional practice and societal understandings of crime and criminal justice. The potential harm associated with risk can lead to uncertainty, fear and conflict as well as disproportionate, ineffective and ill-judged state responses to perceived risk and risky groups. Risk, Crime and Society is a series featuring monographs and edited collections which examine the notion of risk, the risky behaviour of individuals and groups, as well as state responses to risk and its consequences in contemporary society. The series will include critical examinations of the notion of risk and the problematic nature of state responses to perceived risk. While Risk, Crime and Society will consider the problems associated with 'mainstream' risky groups including sex offenders, terrorists and white collar criminals, it welcomes scholarly analysis which broadens our understanding of how risk is defined, interpreted and managed. Risk, Crime and Society examines risk in contemporary society through the multi-disciplinary perspectives of law, criminology and socio-legal studies and will feature work that is theoretical as well as empirical in nature.

More information about this series at
http://www.palgrave.com/gp/series/14593

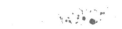

Joanna Large

The Consumption of Counterfeit Fashion

palgrave
macmillan

Joanna Large
School for Policy Studies
University of Bristol
Bristol, UK

Palgrave Studies in Risk, Crime and Society
ISBN 978-3-030-01330-1   ISBN 978-3-030-01331-8   (eBook)
https://doi.org/10.1007/978-3-030-01331-8

Library of Congress Control Number: 2018959444

This Palgrave Pivot imprint is published by the registered company Springer Nature
Switzerland AG
The registered company address is: Gewerbestrasse 11, 6330 Cham, Switzerland

ACKNOWLEDGMENTS

This book comes from a number of years of interest in the counterfeit fashion industry, and, even long before getting to the stage of wanting to write it, so many colleagues and friends have helped me along the way – through discussing ideas, support and at times, simply some encouragement. My first thanks go to the staff and my PhD supervisory team in the School of Law at Leeds University. This opportunity has made everything since possible. During the writing of this book, I moved from the School of Social Sciences and Law at Teesside University to the School for Policy Studies at University of Bristol. I would like to thank my colleagues in both departments for their support and encouragement. I also have to thank my wider criminological academic (and also support) network, who inspire me academically and make the tough days easier: Alexandra Hall, James Treadwell, Tom Raymen, Tammy Ayres, Oliver Smith and Corina Medley. Thank you to everyone who has contributed to my research.

Writing this book during increasingly pressurised times in HE, not to mention long distance job and house moves and various personal life 'mini crises' would simply not have been possible without the support of my friends and family who are too many to mention individually: I love you all. Special thanks to Scottish Katie for believing in me and being the kindest, toughest yet most gentle person to ever walk into my life, to the JSAM crew for the 'moments', Charlene for the headspace, and of course; mum, dad, Sophie and Mick for being my rocks.

CONTENTS

CHAPTER 1

Turning Criminological Attention to Counterfeit Fashion

Abstract Changes in how we consume, impacted by developments in technology and global travel, have transformed the consumption of fashion. As the industry continues to grow, and opportunities to consume fashion develop and expand, increasing concern has been afforded to the illicit counterfeit fashion industry. These concerns highlight the potential economic damage of counterfeit branded goods in terms of intellectual property rights infringements, and, the recognition that counterfeit production and supply provides a low risk and high profit opportunity for funding criminal lifestyles and activities. This chapter introduces the issue of fashion counterfeiting, outlines the context of the book and argues the need for a more critical exploration of the consumption of counterfeit fashion.

Keywords Fashion industry • Counterfeits • Illicit markets • Demand and supply

INTRODUCTION

The global fashion industry is booming. A fundamental piece of the cultural and economic consumer picture, the apparel and footwear sector was valued at $1.7 trillion dollars in 2017 (Euromonitor 2018). Despite cries of the 'death of the high street' and several big fashion brands running

J. Large, *The Consumption of Counterfeit Fashion*, Palgrave Studies in Risk, Crime and Society,
https://doi.org/10.1007/978-3-030-01331-8_1

1

into financial trouble in recent years, the industry is remarkably adept at adapting, evolving and flourishing even in times of global financial crises (see European Commission 2018). Changes in how we consume, largely impacted by developments in technology and global travel, on the one hand have manipulated when and how we consume fashion, yet on the other hand, perpetuate and increase our desire to consume fashion. As the industry continues to grow, and opportunities to consume fashion develop and expand, increasing concern has been afforded to the illicit counterfeit fashion industry. These concerns largely have rested with the economic damage counterfeit branded goods have in terms of intellectual property rights infringements, yet, further lie with the recognition that counterfeit production and supply provides a low risk and high profit opportunity for funding criminal lifestyles and activities.

Reflecting the nature of the international trade, the trade in counterfeit goods is a globally complex network which spans international borders, diverse legal systems, not to mention competing policy priorities. Although there has been increasing recognition from regulatory and law enforcement officials nationally and internationally regarding the 'growing problem' of counterfeiting, academic criminology in the large part has been somewhat slow in addressing the issue (Yar 2005; Wall and Large 2010; Large 2015; Hall and Antonopoulos 2016; Sullivan et al. 2016; Antonopoulos et al. 2017). This is particularly evident with the specific issue of fashion goods that are often described as 'non-safety critical' counterfeits (see Yar 2005). Understanding the consumption of, and trade in, counterfeit fashion goods proves troublesome for traditional boundaries of criminology. On the one hand, this is due to the differing legal statuses associated within the counterfeit transaction: – for example within England and Wales under the Trade Marks Act 1994, manufacturing or retailing a counterfeit product is considered a criminal offence; yet purchasing the counterfeit (at least for personal use) is not necessarily. However, buying a counterfeit is, in the large part, positioned as deviant and problematic. Therefore, a considerable emphasis of anti-counterfeiting policy attempts to convince potential consumers why not to buy counterfeit (see Large 2015). On the other hand, counterfeiting, especially of fashion products, is considered as a less pressing priority on the criminological agenda, that is no doubt related to its definition as 'non-safety critical' counterfeiting and perception as a 'victimless' crime (Anderson 1999; Patent Office 2004).

A Background to Counterfeiting

To set the scene, counterfeiting, along with piracy has been described as the most financially valuable trade in illicit goods for 'transnational criminals' (May 2017). A report by Global Financial Integrity estimates the retail value of counterfeits at $923 billion to $1.13 trillion US dollars (May 2017: xi). Other estimations include that of the Organisation for Economic Co-Operation and Development (OECD) who in April 2016 suggested that the global import trade in counterfeit goods amounts to nearly half a trillion US dollars (OECD and EUIPO 2016). Another common estimation suggests counterfeiting makes up approximately five to seven percent of all world trade, although the empirical basis for this claim is not clear (see Spink and Fejes 2012). The OECD, however, does estimate that approximately five percent of imports into the European Union (EU) are counterfeit (OECD and EUIPO 2016). The range of counterfeit products traded, reflects the diversity of products and items in the legal marketplace. As one law enforcement official in research by Antonopoulos et al. (2018) on the financial aspects of the trade in counterfeit products suggests:

> There are two categories for the things that are counterfeited. There is everything and there is anything.... (Interview with Police Intellectual Property Crime Unit Officer cited in Antonopoulos et al. 2018: 1)

In terms of the global flows of counterfeit goods, China is recognised as the main source for counterfeit goods that enter the EU, with Chinese origin counterfeits making up 66 percent of the volume of the goods detained at EU borders (European Commission DG TAXUD[1]). Other countries of special concern to the European Commission (EC) include India for pharmaceutical products and Turkey for cosmetics and perfume. In 2013, customs seized EUR 26.1 million worth of cosmetics and perfumes originating from Turkey alone. These figures suggest that although China may well be the biggest player in the production of counterfeit goods, it is by far from the only source of goods. Notably, China, although suggested to be the source country for over two thirds of counterfeit goods circulating in the EU, it is also where most of the legal goods

[1] Directorate General for Customs and Taxation Union, European Commission.

circulating in the EU are also produced (Europol and OHIM 2016). The prominence of China, and also Turkey, as legitimate importers is an important point to consider in any assessment of illicit counterfeit markets. The parallel nature of counterfeit trade is highly relevant (see Rojek 2017 for a discussion), as is the recognition of the temporal, spatial and cultural definitions of legal and illegal activity (see Hudson 2019). These points will be returned to shortly.

A Note of Caution on Trends Data

Much of what we know about the scope and trends of counterfeiting comes from various official, trade and industry sources. However, despite the wide citation of statistics on the size of the industry, so much so that Spink and Fejes (2012: 258) suggest they have achieved 'mythological stature', caution does need to be exercised with their accuracy. Spink and Fejes (2012) identified how statements about the size of the industry can be traced back primarily to three documents. In reviewing these 'core reference documents (CIB 1997; OECD 2007; FBI 2002)' they noted:

> The two full reports – CIB 1997 and OECD 2007 – emphasized the challenges of developing both a sound methodology and a data gathering process to provide a statistically supported estimate. The FBI (2002) reference was a one page release with no reference to the methodology used for the estimate. Conversely, while the two full reports were substantial and had a developed methodological foundation, they clearly stated that the methodology was, at best, an educated guess. (Spink and Fejes 2012: 265)

Customs seizure data underpins most official estimations on the trade and although those sophisticated techniques may quantify the economic impact of counterfeiting (see OECD and EUIPO 2016), caution is needed. Valuation estimations are based on assumptions about the product and consumer, which as explored in forthcoming chapters, are often problematic. Seizure data may provide ideas about goods seized, frequency of seizure and origin and destination information, however, it does have the potential to be skewed for a number of reasons (see Large 2019). Additionally, customs data does not help us understand the domestic market for counterfeit goods, nor, intricacies and nuances in the local and global supply and demand of counterfeit goods.

The Nature of Counterfeit Goods

One of the common ways of describing the nature of counterfeit goods is to refer to their 'safety' in relation to their potential physical harms to the consumer. The tendency here is to separate goods into a distinction of 'safety critical' or 'non-safety critical' (see Yar 2005). Non-safety critical goods such as clothing and fashion items (Wall and Large 2010; Treadwell 2012; Large 2015) that appear relatively harmless to the consumer are available, as are safety critical goods that can pose serious health and safety consequences such as vehicle/airline parts (Yar 2005); defence products (Sullivan and Wilson 2017); food, alcohol and tobacco (Antonopoulos 2009; McEwan and Straus 2009; Shen et al. 2010; Lord et al. 2017; Shen and Antonopoulos 2017) and pharmaceuticals (Hall and Antonopoulos 2016; Hall et al. 2017) amongst other things. For some, this justifies a concern about some types of counterfeits more so than others. This distinction between types of counterfeit goods may provide a useful broadly contextual starting point, however it is important to not treat these as binary or mutually exclusive categories. For example, seemingly 'safe' leather fashion goods may be treated with toxic chemicals or sunglasses may have no adequate UV protection. Further, this kind of conception of counterfeit goods places a clear emphasis on *consumer* safety with an assumption that the consumer faces the biggest risk of victimisation when buying substandard goods. Following this, an implicit assumption can be made that the next 'victim' may be the legitimate retailer whose brand might be harmed if consumers are put off buying their products due to negative experiences with counterfeits. Other conceptions of harm and victimisation however, might consider broader environmental risks: for example, mass production of clothing using toxic chemicals, which may or may not be directly harmful to humans but have considerable impacts on the environment. Given the concerns about levels of toxicity and use of chemicals in clothing sold by legitimate retailers (see for example Khan and Malik 2013; Brooks 2015; Greenpeace 2016) it is likely that counterfeit fashion products may also have underestimated *safety* concerns. The problem with conceptualising safety in this way is that it underplays issues around producer, worker and various supply conditions, not to mention environmental harm, tending to reinforce more traditional notions of victimisation and crime. This issue is explored more fully in Chap. 4.

Deception and Quality

Although the type of counterfeit product may have inherent implications for physical harm to the consumer or user, there are two further distinctions related to the nature of the product which are also relevant: deception and quality. These distinctions can have important implications for estimating the value and economic impact of the counterfeit market. Early economic accounts of counterfeiting describe the market as based on deceptive – where consumers buy counterfeits in the belief they are the genuine product, and non-deceptive – where consumers are willing and complicit in the purchase of counterfeits (Grossman and Shapiro 1988). It is too simplistic to assume that the whole market for counterfeit goods is based on deceiving unaware buyers, as much as the same can be said that all buyers will know, or at least suspect, that a good they have been sold is a counterfeit. This is true within various stages of the supply chain as much as it for the end consumer market. The idea that deception can be described in a binary manner is also problematic – more useful is Bosworth's (2006) scale of 'super deceptive to completely non-deceptive'. We also know that the quality of counterfeits can vary hugely, and a scaled approach is again more helpful. These ranges in deception and quality are evident across counterfeit product type.

Given in most jurisdictions the legislative framework criminalises the manufacture and supply of counterfeits, not to mention the potential for greater profits if a seller can deceive a buyer into buying a counterfeit at the cost of the genuine item, it can be assumed that in the large part the seller openly advertising they are selling counterfeits is often (but not always) low. Therefore, making distinctions in relation to factors of deception and quality relies on making assumptions about counterfeit products and often, the consumer. There may be a tendency to place the responsibility onto the consumer to make a judgement on a products' (potential lack of) authenticity via the situation surrounding its supply and the products quality. However, quality is a difficult aspect to establish at the time of purchase – a problem exacerbated by the increase in online shopping. To avoid deceptive sales, various campaigns encouraging consumers to recognise when a good might be counterfeit exist, yet, as explored by Large (2015) there are a number of reasons why consumers may still be misled into buying a counterfeit product.

Exploring the interconnections between deception and quality has been key in much literature related to the harms of counterfeit goods.

Hopkins et al. (2003) devised a Harm Matrix which plots harm in relation to levels of deception and quality (see Fig. 1.1). By typifying goods in this way there is a clear indication that the primary concern related to the harm or problem of counterfeiting is in relation to the consumer, or the brand of the product being counterfeited. This emphasises the point made by Wall and Large (2010: 1095) that counterfeiting does not have 'a clear pattern of victimisation'. Further, it reinforces support for suggesting that counterfeiting (especially in the form of those described as 'non-safety critical' products) can be 'harmless' and therefore considered a 'victimless crime' (Anderson 1999: 56; Patent Office 2004: s4).

However, although much of the anti-counterfeiting argument high-lights the potential of harm to the consumer and the copied brand, harm – or more commonly described in terms such as impact or costs – has been

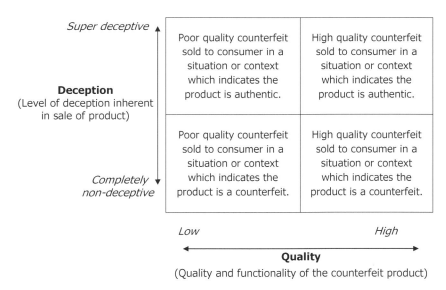

Fig. 1.1 Harm Matrix: level of deception versus quality. (Adapted from Hopkins et al. 2003: 11; Bosworth 2006. Hopkins et al. (2003) have developed the Harm Matrix, however given the recognition of the problems of addressing deception and quality in a binary manner, I have adapted the original matrix to use Bosworth's (2006) scaled approach of super deceptive to completely non-deceptive. I further have adapted the matrix to consider quality on a scaled approach)

flagged in different ways. The OECD (1998) highlights that in addition to the effects on the consumer and intellectual property owner, further socio-economic effects may be felt in terms of impact: slowing innovation and growth, the environment in terms of substandard products and disposal practices, loss of jobs, loss of foreign direct investment, general impacts on trading, impacts on governments in relation to tax losses, costs of dealing with counterfeiting and opportunities for corruption, and finally fostering and facilitating criminal markets and activities. Particular concern relates to the role counterfeiting is said to have in transnational and/or organised crime networks (Europol and EUIPO 2017).

Counterfeiting is recognised as a highly profitable business that is attractive to criminal groups and networks (Shen et al. 2010; Wall and Large 2010; INTERPOL 2014; Large 2015; Hall and Antonopoulos 2016; Europol and EUIPO 2017; Lord et al. 2017; Sullivan and Wilson 2017; Antonopoulos et al. 2018). This is because its high profit potential combines with 'pitifully low sanctions' (AIM 2005: 1) – or at the least numerous challenges in enforcing legislation. Organisations such as the United Nations Office on Drugs and Crime (UNODC) highlight the evidence for 'organised crime groups' being involved in counterfeiting through national and international authorities' attention on counterfeit markets and supply chains. UNODC also identify the 'strategic and operational links between counterfeiting and drug trafficking' for example (UNODC 2013). The Intellectual Property Crime Group (IPCG), based in the United Kingdom, further documents examples of the relationship between counterfeiting and criminal activities citing 'many' cases where links have been found. These 'criminal activities' include 'money laundering, people trafficking, loan sharking and the exploitation of children' (IPCG 2010: 15). Some caution must be placed here towards the uncritical usage of terms such as organised crime and organised crime groups in many of these kinds of documents (see Hobbs 2002; Levi 2007, 2014; Croall 2010), however the nature of the criminal activities and markets is of importance to wider discussions of [dis]organised crime (see Von Lampe 2016).

Although it is possible to make some generalisations about the harm and impact of counterfeiting, it is important to recognise from the outset a 'one size fits all' approach to interrogating counterfeiting as an issue is problematic. Compounding the already noted lack of clear pattern of victimisation, is the nature of the harm of counterfeit products being encapsulated within notions of deception and quality. Therefore, caution needs to be exerted with making distinctions in relation to the nature and types of counterfeit goods. This is, as noted above, is important in relation to safety critical and non-safety critical, deceptive and non-deceptive, high quality and low quality. The nature of counterfeit goods is therefore best considered on a series of continuums (Large 2015; Hall and Antonopoulos 2016; Antonopoulos et al. 2018).

The Concern About Counterfeit Fashion

Counterfeiting has varying definitions and many other terms such as fake, imitation, copy, knock-off, replica and look-alike are often used interchangeably with counterfeit (see Lin 2011). Although some discussion exists regarding the differing definitions of terms like counterfeit and imitation, particularly when it comes to legal processes, the reality is that for the large part these goods cannot be meaningfully separated, to consumers at least, in such way. In many cases, a trade mark infringing good may be infringing other intellectual property laws such as copyright. This book is concerned with one form of product counterfeiting, fashion, and although this is largely encapsulated within trade mark law, there will inevitably be overlap with design piracy and copyright issues. The focus on fashion products exclusively, seemingly 'non-safety critical', reflects a desire to examine issues which appear to pose additional challenges for criminology (Wall and Large 2010) especially in relation to conceptions of crime, victimisation and harm. A broad understanding of fashion is applied which encapsulates the vast range of fashion apparel and accessory products counterfeited: from luxury 'high' fashion to sportswear, T-shirts and accessories such as sunglasses and bags. However, beauty and grooming products such as cosmetics, straightening irons and non-surgical body enhancement products (i.e. Botox) are not included in this definition for the purpose of this book, nor are more general 'fashionable' products such as art, electronics etc.

Fashion counterfeiting complicates arguments in relation to harm and victimisation (Wall and Large 2010) and it is not uncommon to hear authorities and industry groups lamenting the apathetic consumer who fails to see little wrong with buying counterfeit fashion goods. Customs and local authority seizure data confirms high numbers of counterfeit fashion products in national and international markets and a quick search online reinforces more recent concerns about the ease of accessing counterfeit fashion on the internet. Fashion counterfeiting perhaps more so than any other form of counterfeiting is most associated with the image of a 'victimless crime' as the physical harm to consumers more attributable to safety critical goods are not generally evident. Regardless of whether individual members of the public have ever actually purchased (knowingly or not), fashion counterfeits are something we are all familiar with – whether it be knock offs of luxury fashion goods, or copies of Premier League football shirts. Therefore, despite problems with much of the data highlighting the scale of the counterfeit industry and questions about the validity of some of the economic and financial impact claims, it is difficult to dispute that the industry is not huge and providing new and mutating opportunities for criminality (Treadwell 2012; Hall and Antonopoulos 2016; Rojek 2017; Antonopoulos et al. 2018).

THE CONTEXT OF CONSUMPTION

Despite what appears to be a relatively new emphasis of concern and interest in counterfeiting, both from a regulatory and law enforcement perspective and also academically, counterfeiting is not a new phenomenon. What has suggested to have changed is a movement away from a small-scale and relatively localised 'cottage industry' (Vagg and Harris 1998: 189) to a rapidly developing complex global market. Continued rapid advances in technology, most notably the growth of internet banking, online shopping and social media, have transformed the nature of the market(s) for counterfeit goods. It is easier than ever to distribute, produce and manufacture goods (Heinonen et al. 2012; Treadwell 2012; Wilson and Fenoff 2014; Hall and Antonopoulos 2016). In addition, the internet enables a heightened drive and desire for counterfeit (and legitimate) goods more generally (Heinonen et al. 2012; Treadwell 2012; Lavorgna 2014; Wilson and Fenoff 2014; Hall and Antonopoulos 2016; Crewe 2017; Rojek 2017). Alongside technological advancements, the nature of contemporary late capitalism and its resultant impact on consumer culture have all contributed to the rapidly changing nature of illegal markets (Hall et al. 2008; Hall and Antonopoulos 2016).

The focus on the consumption of counterfeit fashion of this book reflects the acknowledgement that the sustainability of illegal markets, such as that of counterfeits, is inherently reliant on the consumption of products (counterfeit or not). This is the case for counterfeit products consumers are deceived into buying, as much as is the case for counterfeits consumers knowingly buy. Yet, we remain in a situation where despite increased attention from criminologists towards understanding the *supply* of counterfeit goods, much of what is known about the consumption (or *demand*) of these goods tends to come from industry sources or outside of criminology (see Large 2019 for a more detailed discussion of this). As a result, the consumption of counterfeit products tends to be understood as something outside of usual consumer behaviour, with an implication that the practice is deviant. This is an important and relevant issue to address when contextualised within anti-counterfeiting policy that places the onus on consumer responsibility – both implicitly and explicitly. In its most simple form the basic presumption of this approach is an assumption that if consumers cease to purchase counterfeits then there will be less demand for the supply of counterfeits. Consumers are told to 'not buy fakes' because they are harmful. Thus, anti-counterfeiting policy tends to be based on generic assumptions about the 'harms' of counterfeiting and a simplistic understanding of consumer behaviour (Large 2015). Criminologists must engage critically with an understanding of why counterfeit markets exist when we know that many consumers knowingly buy counterfeit products. Thus, there is a need to consider demand for illicit goods within the context of consumer capitalism. At the same time, more recognition is needed in the problems with focusing on licit and illicit markets as if they are separate entities (see Hudson 2019 for a good theoretical overview here). This falls into broader concerns of critical criminologists and zemiologists who, having drawn on early critiques of criminological theory, recognise the need to go beyond focusing on crime, and instead situate *harm* as central (see Hillyard et al. 2004; Hall 2012; White 2013; Hall and Winlow 2015; Pemberton 2015; Smith and Raymen 2018; see also Boukli and Kotze 2018).

Given the huge market for counterfeit goods the first assumption which needs to be abandoned is the idea that counterfeit consumption can be typified demographically or as deviant. Through focusing on the end market consumption of counterfeit fashion; a grey area in terms of criminality and a topic on the border of more traditional criminological concern this book is concerned with the embedded nature of harm in consumer capitalism (see Hall et al. 2008; Hall 2012; Hall and Winlow 2015; Smith and Raymen 2018). Situated within this framework, this book aims to provide the first critical account of the consumption of counterfeit fashion.

OVERVIEW AND SYNOPSIS

This book aims to provide the first substantive criminological exploration of the consumption of counterfeit fashion goods. Drawing upon qualitative exploratory research conducted with consumers (including those who did and did not knowingly buy counterfeits) the aim is to provide an understanding of counterfeit fashion consumption from a perspective informed by advances in critical criminology and zemiology (the study of harm). In this book, it is argued if criminology is to understand illicit markets, we need to move beyond simply focusing on the illicit market as if it exists separately and provide a more critical understanding within the context of the parallel legal market. Here I draw on Rojek's (2017) description of counterfeiting as a 'parasitic' industry.

Through transcending traditional notions of crime, criminality and the 'criminal other', the examination of counterfeit fashion as a criminological topic demonstrates many of the limitations of traditional or administrative criminological theory at dealing with contemporary global issues which do not fall neatly within traditional constructs and conceptualisations of crime and victimisation. By focusing on the non-criminal aspect of the counterfeit supply-demand transaction on a topic that on appearance, sits outside of the criminological agenda, a critical exploration of harm and crime can be undertaken. Therefore, this book aims to provide an understanding of the micro dynamics of consumer attitudes and behaviour which are contextualised within the broader socio-political context of consumer capitalism that addresses notions of harm beyond constraints of criminal law. In order to do so, the focus of this book will be on the demand for illicit counterfeit fashion goods; essentially seeking to explore why people buy counterfeit fashion. For context, the book will also examine issues in relation to production and supply of both illicit and licit fashion products more generally.

Chapter 2 provides an exploration of the consumption of counterfeit fashion goods with the aim of challenging popular ideas about the 'typical' counterfeit consumer. The chapter will map out the stereotypical consumer that closely aligns with many of the assumptions held about counterfeit consumption, and through presentation of empirical data, challenge these notions. The chapter will then build on the idea of 'who' buys counterfeit fashion and explore this within a broader contextual discussion about the nature of consuming counterfeit fashion, particularly in terms of examining fundamental assumptions of why people buy counterfeit fashion. This includes situational and contextual factors, such as availability of counterfeit goods and their cost. These discussions consider 'primary markets' (where consumers are deceived into buying counterfeits) and 'secondary markets' (where consumers knowingly buy counterfeits) exploring similarities and differences in those who knowingly and unknowingly buy counterfeit fashion. As part of examining why people do buy counterfeit fashion, this chapter also examines the reasons why people would avoid consuming counterfeits.

Chapter 3 develops an exploration into the understanding of why people buy counterfeit fashion through examining the micro dynamics of consumer purchasing behaviour and attitudes towards the consumption of counterfeit fashion. In this chapter I will argue that although cost, location and other superficial factors have some importance in counterfeit consumption, this only goes part of the way to explain consumption. This presents a challenge to much of the existing work on the demand for counterfeit products. The main thrust of the argument throughout this chapter is that motivations for consuming counterfeit goods need to be contextualised within an understanding about consumption of legitimate fashion goods. This is largely due to the nature of the fashion process being one of 'introduction and imitation'. Not only is the industry based on a continual perpetuation of consumer desire for new products, but the very nature of fashion and the sustainability of consumer industries is inherently based on copying.

Chapter 4 continues to explore the question of why consumers buy counterfeit goods within broader discussions around attitudes towards crime, harm and victimisation. In addition to examining the impacts of the counterfeit industry, this chapter also examines the inter-related nature of the counterfeit and legitimate industry from a social harm perspective. Despite debates about counterfeit goods tending to centre on harm (or lack of harm in some cases), it is clear that ideals of direct and deserving victimisation play an important role in shaping responses towards the debate. Thus, despite the notional focus on harm, it can be argued that these debates fail to engage with a thorough and critical consideration of social harm that moves properly beyond the focus on individual consumers, legitimate business and largescale criminal activity. This chapter problematizes examining counterfeiting within a framework constrained by focusing on crime though expanding the argument that it is problematic to consider the illicit market of counterfeits alone. The chapter argues that counterfeit consumption needs to be understood within the context of the harmful nature of contemporary consumer capitalism.

Chapter 5 reflects on the question that fundamentally underpins the book – why do people consume counterfeit fashion? Despite the evidential importance of the consumer in the counterfeiting realm there has been a lack of attention within criminology about the demand for counterfeit goods (and understanding the dynamics and issues of counterfeit goods trading more generally). A tendency to explain counterfeit consumption through deviance or 'othering'; reinforces stereotypical assumptions about consumers and overplays the importance of superficial factors in consumption. This book seeks to develop a better understanding of why counterfeit markets exist, when we know that many consumers knowingly buy counterfeit products and argues there is a need to consider demand for illicit goods within the context of consumer capitalism; and problematize creating a false distinction between licit and illicit markets and illegal and legal activity. Through focusing on the end market consumption of counterfeit fashion; a grey area in terms of criminality and a topic on the border of more traditional criminological concern, this book is concerned with the embedded nature of harm in consumer capitalism.

INTRODUCING THE RESEARCH PARTICIPANTS

This research is based on research which sought to examine consumer behaviour and attitudes towards counterfeit fashion goods and their motivations, drives and desires for consuming these goods (or not). This research started from the position that as a form of 'non-safety critical' counterfeiting, fashion should be examined separately from other forms of counterfeit goods. This was for a number of reasons. Firstly, as it has been argued elsewhere (Large 2009; Wall and Large 2010; Treadwell 2012) and explored above, non-safety critical counterfeit goods on the surface pose different issues to safety critical counterfeit goods – most notably in relation to direct harm to the consumer. This links to the second reason being that much of the existing knowledge on counterfeiting and its harm tends to be uncritical and generalised across different types of counterfeits. This fails to recognise the nuances and complexities at stake, especially in relation to harm. Finally, this research, being exploratory and interdisciplinary, also sought to understand fashion counterfeiting within a broader context of fashion and consumption. The wider research project this book draws upon utilised a mixed-methods approach that allowed a capturing of the context before examining findings and issues in more depth using qualitative interviews and focus groups. Starting out with limited quality existing knowledge on the area, it was felt useful to employ a self-completion questionnaire to just over 800 members of the public to generate initial thoughts and inform the latter qualitative stages of the research. Therefore, although the survey generated interesting insights into people's attitudes and consumption of counterfeits, the results were considered exploratory and informative and helped primarily for research development. The data in this book, however, draws primarily on 27 qualitative interviews conducted over a four year period with a range of counterfeit and non-counterfeit consumers. Prior to commencing the research, ethical approval was sought and granted from the university's research ethics committee.

Throughout the remainder of the book, different participants will be introduced by way of a short profile. All interview participants lived in the United Kingdom at the time of the research, albeit in a geographically diverse range of locations, and were recruited via several means. These included those who took part in the initial exploratory survey, those recruited via word of mouth and those who responded to interview flyers/adverts in online forums, beauty salons and hairdressers, education buildings, local libraries and various workplaces through using gatekeepers and contacts. As a result, participants came from a range of backgrounds: from undergraduate students, to post graduate research students, to labourers, to service economy employees, to small business owners and fashion designers, and those employed in academic and professional service roles. The youngest interviewee was Poppy, at aged 19 and the oldest was Lucy at 56. All participants have been anonymised in this research and are described using pseudonyms.

It is useful to draw the interview participants into three broad groups: those who have never bought a counterfeit and do not intend to, those who have been deceived (or at least were unsure) into buying a counterfeit, and those who knowingly have – or knowingly would – buy a counterfeit fashion item. By way of introducing the range of consumers in the research, five profiles are described in more detail here. One each from non-consumers (Amelia) and deceived consumers (Charlie), and three from the knowingly have/would buy counterfeits group (Lucy, Alfie, Amy).

Amelia

Amelia is a 21 year old, female, registered as a part time student and part time employed, living just outside of a city in the very South West of England. Amelia described herself as financially struggling at times, yet, still spent a good proportion of her income – as much as £300 some months – on buying fashion items. Amelia was highly interested in fashion, and very conscious of being fashionable. As an active user of online celebrity and fashion forums, Amelia was recruited following initially completing the online survey via a celebrity 'gossip' web forum. Very much against counterfeiting, Amelia had strong views about the harmful and problematic nature of the counterfeit industry.

Charlie

Charlie is a 29 year old male from the East of England. Living with his partner in the small town he had grown up in, Charlie worked as a labourer for the building trade.

Charlie was very much into branded and designer fashion and described how he would only buy items if they were a recognised brand name. Charlie considered himself as fashion conscious and described how he spent quite high amounts on buying fashion items. Charlie, similarly to Amelia, was against counterfeiting and considered it detrimental to the fashion industry. However, on a number of occasions – mostly on holiday – Charlie described how he had been deceived into buying products he later realised to be counterfeit.

Lucy

Lucy is the oldest interview participant at 56 years of age. Lucy, who works in an independent clothing retailer, which sold second hand luxury clothing, in a suburb in Yorkshire, had lots of views on counterfeit fashion largely due to her experiences of coming across fakes at work. Lucy was cautious about the trouble counterfeits could cause if they were accidentally sold in the shop. Lucy had previously knowingly bought counterfeits in the past, however, she described how she would no longer do so – attributing this to the knowledge she had gained as she got older and realised how harmful counterfeiting can be. Lucy considered herself as highly interested in fashion, and saw counterfeiting as damaging to the broader industry, as well as small retailers such as the one she worked for.

Alfie

Alfie is a 38 year old male and during a career break, taking on full time post graduate studies. Alfie described his average spending on fashion items as low – on average less than £50 a month and suggested that he actively rejected buying goods with a luxury or designer brand name. Alfie also identified a number of shops that he would avoid shopping in due to concerns about ethics. Alfie identified as someone who had previously bought counterfeits but attributed this to being in China, were he considered the only goods available were counterfeit. Although Alfie would not buy branded goods, he did describe how in the future he may well be tempted to buy counterfeit goods as a way of taking a stance against "branded culture" and being "anti-fashion".

Amy

Amy is a 22 year old female living in Yorkshire and in the final year of a fashion and design degree. Amy hoped to go on to become a fashion designer following university. Amy described how her spending is currently quite low on fashion – but this was largely due to the limited income as a student and would usually be much higher. Amy described how it was important for her friends and peers to see her as fashionable and she is keen to have the most recently available goods. Amy, perhaps surprisingly for an aspiring fashion designer, actively bought counterfeit goods as a way of associating herself with brands she "loved", yet, would not be able to afford otherwise. Amy disputed that this was harmful to the brand as she recognised that if she could afford to, she would buy the genuine item. Generally, Amy did not see counterfeiting as a particularly harmful issue, and described how she, like other friends, would regularly place orders for specific products they desired.

References

AIM. (2005, April). *Faking It: Why Counterfeiting Matters* (Briefing Paper). Brussels: Association des Industries de Marque. European Brands Association.

Anderson, J. (1999). The Campaign Against Dangerous Counterfeit Goods. In R. E. Kendall (Ed.), *International Criminal Police Review: Special Issue on Counterfeiting*. Lyon: ICPO/Interpol. Available from http://counterfeiting. unicri.it/docs/International%20Criminal%20Police%20Review.pdf. Accessed 13 June 2011.

Antonopoulos, G. A. (2009). Cigarettes of 'Ambiguous Quality' in the Greek Black Market?: Findings from an Empirical Study on Cigarette Smuggling. *Trends in Organised Crime, 12*(3–4), 260–266.

Antonopoulos, G. A., Hall, A., Large, J., & Shen, A. (2017). An Introduction to the Special Issue on Counterfeiting. *Trends in Organised Crime, 20*(3–4), 247–251.

Antonopoulos, G. A., Hall, A., Large, J., Shen, A., Crang, M., & Andrews, M. (2018). *Fake Goods, Real Money. The Counterfeiting Business and Its Financial Management*. Bristol: Policy Press.

Bosworth, D. (2006). *Modelling the Counterfeiting Decision and the Effect of Anti Counterfeiting Policies*. Available from: www.derekbosworth.com. Accessed 27 July 2011.

Boukli, A., & Kotze, J. (Eds.). (2018). *Zemiology: Reconnecting Crime and Social Harm*. London: Palgrave.

Brooks, A. (2015). *Clothing Poverty. The Hidden World of Fast Fashion and Second-Hand Clothes*. London: Zed.

CIB. (1997). *Countering Counterfeiting. A Guide to Protecting & Enforcing Intellectual Property Rights*. London: Counterfeiting Intelligence Bureau [CIB]. International Chamber of Commerce [ICC].

Crewe, L. (2017). *The Geographies of Fashion. Consumption, Space, and Value*. London: Bloomsbury.

Croall, H. (2010). Middle-Range Business Crime. In F. Brookman, M. Maguire, H. Pierpoint, & T. Bennett (Eds.), *Handbook on Crime*. Devon: Willan.

Euromonitor. (2018, April). *World Market for Apparel and Footwear*. Euromonitor International. Available from: http://www.euromonitor.com/world-market-for-apparel-and-footwear/report. Accessed 22 July 2018.

European Commission. (2018). *Fashion and High-End Industries in the EU*. European Commission. Internal Market, Industry, Entrepreneurship and SMEs. Available from https://ec.europa.eu/growth/sectors/fashion/high-end-industries/eu_en. Accessed 22 July 2018.

Europol and EUIPO. (2017). *2017 Situation Report on Counterfeiting and Piracy in the European Union*. Europol and European Union Intellectual Property Office [EUIPO]. Available from https://www.europol.europa.eu/publications-documents/2017-situation-report-counterfeiting-and-piracy-in-european-union. Accessed 07 Dec 2017.

Europol and OHIM [Office for Harmonisation in the Internal Market]. (2016). 2015 Situation Report on Counterfeiting in the European Union. [EXCERPT]. *Trends in Organised Crime, 20*(3–4), 370–382.

Federal Bureau of Investigation [FBI]. (2002, July 17). *The FBI and the U.S. Customs Service Announce the National Intellectual Property Rights Coordination Center's First Conference for Members of Congress and Industry in Washington.* Available from https://archives.fbi.gov/archives/news/pressrel/press-releases/the-federal-bureau-of-investigation-and-the-u.s.-customs-service-today-announced-the-national-intellectual-property-rights-coordination-centers-first-conference-for-members-of-congress-and-industry-in-washington. Accessed 30 Nov 2017.

Greenpeace. (2016, January 25). *Hazardous Chemicals Found in Many Outdoor Clothing Brands.* Greenpeace UK. Available from https://www.greenpeace.org.uk/press-releases/hazardous-chemicals-found-many-outdoor-clothing-brands-20160125/. Accessed 30 Nov 2017.

Grossman, G. M., & Shapiro, C. (1988). Foreign Counterfeiting of Status Goods. *The Quarterly Journal of Economics, 103*(1), 79–100.

Hall, S. (2012). *Theorizing Crime and Deviance. A New Perspective.* London: Sage.

Hall, A., & Antonopoulos, G. A. (2016). *Fake Meds Online. The Internet and the Transnational Market in Illicit Pharmaceuticals.* Basingstoke: Palgrave.

Hall, S., & Winlow, S. (2015). *Revitalizing Criminological Theory. Towards a New Ultra-Realism.* London: Routledge.

Hall, S., Winlow, S., & Ancrum, C. (2008). *Criminal Identities and Consumer Culture. Crime, Exclusion and the New Culture of Narcissism.* Devon: Willan.

Hall, A., Koenraadt, R., & Antonopoulos, G. A. (2017). Illicit Pharmaceutical Networks in Europe: Organising the Illicit Medicine Market in the United Kingdom and the Netherlands. *Trends in Organised Crime, 20*(3–4), 296–315.

Heinonen, J. A., Holt, T. J., & Wilson, J. M. (2012). Product Counterfeits in the Online Environment: An Empirical Assessment of Victimization and Reporting Characteristics. *International Criminal Justice Review, 22*(4), 353–371.

Hillyard, P., Pantazis, C., Tombs, S., & Gordon, D. (Eds.). (2004). *Beyond Criminology. Taking Harm Seriously.* London: Pluto.

Hobbs, D. (2002). The Firm: Organisational Logic and Criminal Culture on a Shifting Terrain. *British Journal of Criminology, 42*(1), 549–560.

Hopkins, D. M., Kontnik, L., & Turnage, M. (2003). *Counterfeiting Exposed. Protecting Your Brand and Consumers.* Hoboken: John Wiley and Sons.

Hudson, R. (2019). Economic Geographies of the (Il)Legal and the (Il)Licit. In T. Hall & V. Scalia (Eds.), *A Research Agenda in Global Crime.* London: Edward Elgar.

INTERPOL. (2014). *Against Organised Crime.* Interpol Trafficking and Counterfeiting Case Book 2014. Available from: https://www.interpol.int/

Crime-areas/Trafficking-in-illicit-goods-and-counterfeiting/Trafficking-in-illicit-goods-and-counterfeiting. Accessed 04 Jan 2018.

IPCG. (2010). *Intellectual Property Crime Report 2009–2010*. Intellectual Property Crime Group [IPCG]. UK Intellectual Property Office. Available from: http://www.ipo.gov.uk/ipcreport09.pdf. Accessed 15 Aug 2011.

Khan, S., & Malik, A. (2013). Environmental and Health Effects of Textile Industry Wastewater. In A. Malik, E. Grohmann, & R. Akhtar (Eds.), *Environmental Deterioration and Human Health. Natural and Anthropogenic Determinants*. Dordrecht: Springer.

Large, J. (2009). Consuming counterfeits: exploring assumptions about fashion counterfeiting. In *Papers from the British Society of Criminology Conference 2009. 9*. Available from: http://www.britsoccrim.org/volume9/Frontpages09.pdf. Accessed 15 Aug 2011.

Large, J. (2015). 'Get Real Don't Buy Fakes'. Fashion Fakes and Flawed Policy: The Problem with Taking a Consumer – Responsibility Approach to Reducing the Problem of Counterfeiting. *Criminology and Criminal Justice, 15*(2), 169–185.

Large, J. (2019). The Demand for Counterfeiting on the Criminological Research Agenda. In T. Hall & V. Scalia (Eds.), *A Research Agenda for Global Crime*. Cheltenham: Edward Elgar.

Lavorgna, A. (2014). The Online Trade in Counterfeit Pharmaceuticals: New Criminal Opportunities, Trends and Challenges. *European Journal of Criminology*. First Published Online on November 5 2014 as https://doi.org/10.1177/1477370814554722.

Levi, M. (2007). Organised Crime and Terrorism. In M. Maguire, R. Morgan, & R. Reiner (Eds.), *The Oxford Handbook of Criminology* (4th ed.). Oxford: Oxford University Press.

Levi, M. (2014). Thinking About Organised Crime. *The RUSI Journal, 159*(1), 6–14.

Lin, Y. J. (2011). *Fake Stuff: China and the Rise of Counterfeit Goods*. London: Routledge.

Lord, N., Spencer, J., Bellotti, E., & Benson, K. (2017). A Script Analysis of the Distribution of Counterfeit Alcohol Across Two European Jurisdictions. *Trends in Organised Crime, 20*(3–4), 252–272.

May, C. (2017). *Transnational Crime and the Developing World*. Washington, DC: Global Financial Integrity [GFI]. Available from http://www.gfintegrity.org/wp-content/uploads/2017/03/Transnational_Crime-final.pdf. Accessed 01 Dec 2017.

McEwan, A., & Straus, L. (2009). Counterfeit Tobacco in London: Local Crime Requires an International Solution. *Trends in Organised Crime, 12*(3), 251–259.

OECD. (1998). *The Economic Impact of Counterfeiting*. Organisation for Economic Co-Operation and Development [OECD]. Available from: http://www.oecd.org/dataoecd/11/11/2090589.pdf. Accessed 27 July 2011.

OECD. (2007 [2008]). *The Economic Impact of Counterfeiting and Piracy*. Paris: Organisation for Economic Co-Operation and Development [OECD]. Available from http://www.oecd.org/sti/ind/theeconomicimpactofcounter-feitingandpiracy.htm. Accessed 30 Nov 2017.

OECD and EUIPO. (2016). *Global Trade in Fake Goods Worth Nearly Half a Trillion Dollars a Year*. Organisation for Economic Co-Operation and Development [OECD] and European Union Intellectual Property Office [EUIPO]. Available from http://www.oecd.org/industry/global-trade-in-fake-goods-worth-nearly-half-a-trillion-dollars-a-year.htm. Accessed 22 Oct 2016.

Patent Office [Now Known as the UK Intellectual Property Office]. (2004). *Counter Offensive: An IP Crime Strategy*. Department for Trade and Industry (DTI). Available from: http://www.ipo.gov.uk/ipcrimestrategy.pdf. Accessed 12 June 2011.

Pemberton, S. (2015). *Harmful Societies. Understanding Social Harm*. Bristol: Policy Press.

Rojek, C. (2017). Counterfeit Commerce; Relations of Production, Distribution and Exchange. *Cultural Sociology, 11*(1), 28–43.

Shen, A., & Antonopoulos, G. A. (2017). 'No Banquet Can Do Without Liquor': Alcohol Counterfeiting in the People's Republic of China. *Trends in Organised Crime, 20*(3–4), 273–295.

Shen, A., Antonopoulos, G. A., & von Lampe, K. (2010). "The Dragon Breathes Smoke": Cigarette Counterfeiting in the People's Republic of China. *British Journal of Criminology, 50*(2), 239–258.

Smith, O., & Raymen, T. (2018). Deviant Leisure: A Criminological Perspective. *Theoretical Criminology, 22*(1), 63–82.

Spink, J., & Fejes, Z. L. (2012). A Review of the Economic Impact of Counterfeiting and Piracy Methodologies and Assessment of Currently Utilized Estimates. *International Journal of Comparative and Applied Criminal Justice, 36*(4), 249–271.

Sullivan, B. A., & Wilson, J. M. (2017). An Empirical Examination of Product Counterfeiting Crime Impacting the U.S. Military. *Trends in Organised Crime., 20*(3–4), 316–337.

Sullivan, B. A., Chan, F., Fenoff, R., & Wilson, J. M. (2016). Assessing the Developing Knowledge Base of Product Counterfeiting: A Content Analysis of Four Decades of Research. *Trends in Organised Crime, 20*(3–4), 338–369.

Treadwell, J. (2012). From the Car Boot to Booting It Up? eBay, Online Counterfeit Crime and the Transformation of the Criminal Marketplace. *Criminology and Criminal Justice, 12*(2), 175–192.

UNODC [United Nations Office on Drugs and Crime]. (2013). Counterfeit Products. Excerpt from The Globalization of Crime: A Transnational Organized Crime Threat Assessment, 2010. *Trends in Organised Crime, 16*, 114–124.

Vagg, J., & Harris, J. (1998). Bad Goods: Product Counterfeiting and Enforcement Strategies. In M. Gill (Ed.), *Crime at Work Vol. 2: Increasing the Risk for Offenders*. London: Perpetuity.

von Lampe, K. (2016). *Organised Crime. Analysing Illegal Activities, Criminal Structures & Extra Legal Governance*. London: Sage.

Wall, D. S., & Large, J. (2010). Jailhouse Frocks: Locating the Public Interest in Policing Counterfeit Luxury Fashion Goods. *British Journal of Criminology, 50*(6), 1094–1116.

White, R. (2013). *Environmental Harm: An Eco-Justice Perspective*. Bristol: Policy Press.

Wilson, J. M., & Fenoff, R. (2014). Distinguishing Counterfeit from Authentic Product Retailers in the Virtual Marketplace. *International Criminal Justice Review, 24*(1), 39–58.

Yar, M. (2005). A Deadly Faith in Fakes: Trademark Theft and the Global Trade in Counterfeit Automotive Components. *Internet Journal of Criminology*. www.internetjournalofcriminology.com

CHAPTER 2

The Myth of the 'Deviant Other': Who Buys Fashion Counterfeits?

Abstract This chapter situates an understanding of the consumption of counterfeit fashion goods with the aim of challenging popular ideas about the 'typical' counterfeit consumer and argues that there is little evidence to support this notion. The chapter examines the relevance of situational and contextual factors such as availability of counterfeit goods and their cost. These discussions consider 'primary markets' (where consumers are deceived into buying counterfeits) and 'secondary markets' (where consumers knowingly buy counterfeits), exploring similarities and differences in those who knowingly and unknowingly buy counterfeit fashion. As part of examining why people do buy counterfeit fashion, this chapter also examines the reasons why people would avoid consuming counterfeits.

Keywords Typical counterfeit consumer • Demand for counterfeits • Price • Counterfeit consumption

INTRODUCTION

> We recognise that a small proportion of UK consumers believe it is acceptable to purchase counterfeit goods (IPO 2016: 28).

This statement from the United Kingdom's Intellectual Property (IP) enforcement strategy suggests that those who buy counterfeit goods are

© The Author(s) 2019
J. Large, *The Consumption of Counterfeit Fashion*, Palgrave Studies in Risk, Crime and Society,
https://doi.org/10.1007/978-3-030-01331-8_2

different to the majority of other consumers. This position, which sees counterfeit consumption as 'other', is common in policy and regulatory documentation, and also consumer behaviour research. This tends to be in two ways. The first is the idea that there is a typical counterfeit consumer who can be described by their demographic characteristics. The tendency has been to describe them as 'young' with 'lower income' (Ledbury Research 2007). This falls into broader perceptions that the main reason people buy counterfeits is because they are 'cheap'. The second interpretation is that counterfeit consumers hold different norms and values to non-counterfeit consumers implying they are 'deviant'; this is evident in descriptions of non-counterfeit consumers as the 'law-abiding majority'.

This chapter therefore situates an understanding of the consumption of counterfeit fashion goods with the aim of challenging popular ideas about the 'typical' counterfeit consumer although investigating commonly held assumptions about counterfeit consumption. Through drawing on exploratory data from consumers of counterfeit goods, the chapter examines situational and contextual factors, such as availability of counterfeit goods and their cost. These discussions consider 'primary markets' (where consumers are deceived into buying counterfeits) and 'secondary markets' (where consumers knowingly buy counterfeits) (OECD 2007) in terms of levels of deception inherent in their sale. Finally, this chapter will examine the value in attempts to typify and generalise counterfeit consumption and set out the problems with the notion that counterfeit consumers should be considered as 'deviant' or 'other'.

The Typical Counterfeit Consumer?

The perception of a 'typical fake-buyer' is usually based around lower income consumers, perhaps young and single. The presumption is also that these individuals spend little in all categories and, as a result, are of proportionately limited interest to luxury brand owners (Ledbury Research 2007: 9).

Counterfeit consumers are commonly presented as different from non-counterfeit consumers. This tends to be caught up within assumptions surrounding why people buy counterfeit goods; either because they cannot afford the *real* item, or, because they hold different values about acceptable behaviour. This places an implication on counterfeit buyers as deviant – or at least different. However, those presumed to be an unknowing – or deceived – counterfeit consumer tend to be presented as a victim who has been 'duped' or misled into buying the counterfeit. This consumer may not realise until after the purchase, if indeed at all, that the item they have bought is a fake. Thus, we see a dichotomous presentation of counterfeit consumers emerging from policy and anti-counterfeiting discourse: the victim and the deviant. However, this polemic view is problematic, and not realistic in practice when in policy, even those presumed as victims of counterfeiting are expected to take some responsibility for their actions to minimise their chances of being misled when buying goods (see Large 2015).

From a policy perspective concerned with demand, those who knowingly buy counterfeit goods can be considered the most problematic in one sense, as these consumers are seen to willingly perpetuate market supply. Tackling counterfeit supply through reducing consumer demand therefore, is considered a key enforcement strategy. For these kinds of strategies to be successful it is recognised an understanding of counterfeiting consumption is necessary and this has generated a number of studies which seek to understand counterfeit consumption. One of the main foci of this kind of research is to identify whether counterfeit consumers have any defining characteristics or can be characterised in particular ways. However, this often tends to play into assumptions about who buys counterfeits and why. The idea of a typical counterfeit buyer appears caught up in popular stereotypes of the young and working class. For example, the image of the 'Burberry Chav' was popularised in the media and popular culture in the mid-2000s and was associated with an influx of poor quality counterfeit Burberry products on the marketplace (see Bothwell 2005 'Burberry versus the Chavs', BBC News. For discussions of 'Chavs' see work by Hayward and Yar 2006; Jones 2011). In contrast with these stereotypical images, counterfeit fashion consumers in the research, however, came from many different walks of life; spanned demographic categories, and further, clothing and fashion preferences – much the same as the non-counterfeit consumers. Many counterfeit consumers certainly did not fit into the 'younger, less educated and earn less income' category described by Tom et al. (1998: 419). This tendency to construct counterfeit consumers as 'Other' (Rutter and Bryce 2008: 1149), therefore, appears to bear little relationship to the reality of counterfeit consumption (Ledbury Research 2006, 2007; Rutter and Bryce 2008; Large 2015). As Ledbury Research (2007: 9) summarise 'there is very little to distinguish demographically between those who have bought a fake and those that have not'.

It is likely that the emphasis on *costs* in counterfeit consumption is caught up in assumptions about both social class and financial power. The idea that consumers buy counterfeit because they cannot *afford* to buy genuine goods is evident in both general discourse around counterfeits and anti-counterfeiting policy. However, as with other forms of demo-graphic characteristics, there is little solid evidence to suggest that low income increases propensity and/or desire to purchase counterfeit fashion (ACG 2003; Ledbury Research 2006, 2007; Large 2015). This is not to dispute there is not some sort of financial relevance to counterfeit transac-tions – certainly in the case of the most expensive and exclusive high-end luxury products – it is difficult to see how the majority of regular income consumers can afford them, when the product may well cost a consider-able portion of their monthly or even annual income. This is the whole point of the exclusivity brands are seeking to achieve. However, the range of counterfeit products is much broader than this, likewise, is the range of counterfeit consumers.

'People Buy Counterfeits Because They Are Cheap'

The emphasis on (lower) costs of counterfeits draws on traditional eco-nomic utility theories of supply and demand which sees consumers as rational, cost concerned thinkers who will buy more of something if costs are low, and less when costs are high (Douglas and Isherwood 1996: 6). Although evidence supports 'cheapness' or the 'price advantages' offered by counterfeits as an important factor in their consumption (Bloch et al. 1993; BASCAP 2009; Large 2015), exploring this in explanation in more depth suggests that counterfeit fashion consumption (much like fashion consumption) is not so straightforward. Although product price may be relevant, it is not usually the sole factor driving the motivation for actually *wanting* the product. Additionally, even when cost or 'cheapness' is really important for a consumer, this does not mean that we should attribute this to a consumers' [low] income levels. With a nod to consumer demand focused anti-counterfeiting policy, as a side note, just because people buy counterfeits because they are 'cheap' also does not mean that it should be assumed that all consumers will be able to (or *should* be able to) recognise a product is potentially counterfeit because of its (cheaper) price (Large 2015).

In the first instance we are posed with the subjective nature of what constitutes something being 'cheap'. What is cheap for one person may be expensive for another. For counterfeit goods, the cost of the good should also be considered in relative terms to the genuine product, but also factors such as the products quality and how it is being sold. For example, one research participant Oliver (29 year old, full time employed male, who described himself as 'fashion conscious', spending around £100–£200 a month on apparel/accessories) described how he thought some trainers he bought off the internet were counterfeit because they were being sold at £60. This compared to their usual retail price of around £250. Yet for some people £60 may be considered expensive when value retailers sell trainers for around £10, and even well-known sports brands' trainers can be purchased around £30 or less.

Reflecting emphasis on the counterfeit being a cheaper alternative, two of the research participants, Ruby (21 year old full time student, who described herself as 'fashion conscious' and although only spending around £50 a month on apparel/accessories recognised this was largely due to current limited disposable income) and Amy (22 year old, full time fashion and design student – much like Ruby, described her current low level of spending – £50 or less a month on fashion – due to being a student) described how counterfeits allowed them to buy versions of products they could not otherwise afford. As 'knowing' counterfeit consumers it is difficult to consider Ruby or Amy as contributing towards 'lost sales' of the genuine alternative given that both would have bought the original if they could have afforded it. The counterfeit version provided a way to access something otherwise unobtainable at that point in time. This fits with the broader view that within the context of hyper-consumption, consumers feel that they have some form of 'right' to be able to participate in fashion regardless of their financial means (Hayward 2004). In this sense a counterfeit becomes a logical and rational choice: a means to have something which you would not be able to otherwise have and ultimately serves a purpose in consumption. This manner of thinking is summed up by a young non-counterfeit consumer in the qualitative response section of the exploratory survey research:

> I think fashion fakes are good in a way because some people may not be able to afford the real deal so a fake is the next best thing. So if it makes you happy and confident – does it really matter if it is real or not? (16 year old, female, non-counterfeit buyer)

This perspective fits with the narrative of the young, low income counterfeit consumer. However, in some peer groups being seen with counterfeits because you cannot afford the real thing may be socially stigmatizing and actually serve to ostracise young people in competitive environments. Archer et al.'s (2007) work on young working-class people's identities in relation to consumer goods and education aspiration highlights the fundamental role that consumer products and branded fashion items have (Archer et al. 2007; see also Hall et al. 2008). Incidentally, shaming tactics such as "I buy real" style campaigns (see http://www.ibuyreal.org/) may only serve to exclude and alienate certain groups of consumers. At the same time, socially stigmatizing counterfeits, based on their cheap nature may not be especially productive given the 'social acceptability' (Ledbury Research 2007) of counterfeit goods. Even the counterfeit 'purse parties' of the late 1990s and early 2000s in the United States described by Phillips (2005) where 'buying counterfeit bags has become part of the social whirl in polite society' with 'upscale people' from 'good neighbourhoods' inviting their friends round, along with suppliers of counterfeit bags, and, (similar to the 'Tupperware party', or the 'Ann Summers party'), the host is rewarded for the sales made at the party with a counterfeit bag (to the value of 10 percent) of the income generated (2005: 48–49) suggest that the idea of counterfeits only being appealing to lower income consumers as hugely outdated. Counterfeits have appeal to 'knowing' consumers because of their price advantages regardless of income status. In a similar vein, 'unknowing' or 'unsure' counterfeit consumers may also have bought a product that they suspect to be counterfeit because it was cheap.

Thinking about consumption habits more broadly, when deciding whether to buy something for many consumers price is an important factor. Decision modelling explanations of consumer behaviour posit that several formal rules or strategies guide the decision process. This may be through some form of 'scoring' between or across various product factors (such as price, quality, image) (Yurchisin and Johnson 2010). In this sense, the cost of an item may on the one hand be used as a 'formal decision rule' – weighed up against the products quality and image – or on the other hand as a 'heuristic' – indicators which act as a 'speedy decision' maker (Solomon and Rabolt 2004: 367 in Yurchisin and Johnson 2010). Although a higher price may for some signify better quality, the huge growth in value retailing and 'fast fashion' has changed consumer perceptions towards shopping for 'bargains' and cheap fashion (Morgan and Birtwistle 2009; Yurchisin and Johnson 2010). As Yurchisin and Johnson

(2010: 47) argue 'consumers are now proud to say that they got a good deal on a desired apparel item'. A low price therefore, might indicate poorer quality, but in an era of consuming more and the acceptability of disposable fashion, this is not necessarily a problem.

Although seemingly logical, the main problem with this kind of modelling is the assumption that most fashion purchasing (and by default fashion counterfeit purchasing) is conducted within a rational process, or as Yurchisin and Johnson (2010) describe, 'normative' fashion consumption. Although this may be the case when a consumer functionally *needs* something in particular – a new pair of jeans, or a new dress for an occasion – when a consumer is more likely to 'shop around' for the most suitable product, discussing shopping and consumption with consumers highlights that most consumption of fashion is a result of unplanned buying. As a counter to this position, for example, Yurchisin and Johnson (2010: 80) advocators of a decision modelling process, do acknowledge that consumers engage with impulsive buying however they suggest this is an 'exception to the rational consumer decision process model'. Focusing on factors like cost surely give a superficial explanation of fashion consumption: counterfeit or not. For example, Lucy (56 year old female who worked in a local dress shop – although Lucy had previously purchased counterfeits willingly she was now of the view that counterfeiting is damaging to the fashion industry and small businesses – such as the one she now worked for) recalled one of the times she bought a counterfeit bag although on holiday.

> It was a cheap bag and I liked it. So, I bought it and I thought well it's only a few quid … . It was 10 Euros, so I just bought it. (Lucy)

At first it appears that the fact the bag was 'cheap' was important for why she bought it. However, the purchase was clearly impulsive and unplanned. Although Lucy makes the point it was a 'cheap bag' an important factor not to forget is that she "*liked*" it. Thus, although this appears a logical reasoning of a rational consumer weighing up the price advantages of a product, what the price cannot explain is why she wants the product. Although price may well be an important factor in someone's decision whether to actually go ahead and buy a product it does not explain why the consumer wants to have that product (counterfeit or genuine) in the first place. Here a broader interpretation of consumption is needed.

The Situational Context of Counterfeit Consumption

Although the cost advantages of a counterfeit may provide part of an explanation for their popularity with consumers, it is also likely that the context of their consumption is relevant. The situation and context of the consumption seems to impact on availability and access to counterfeits; concerns about risk, ethics and legality; and characteristics of leisure. Alongside assumptions about the 'cheapness' of counterfeits are common conceptions about where they are purchased. Traditionally, counterfeit sales were primarily associated with market traders and hidden black markets. Growths in international travel provided an expansion of opportunities for consumers to purchase (knowingly and unknowingly) counterfeit products and the once 'exotic symbol' of expensive long-haul travel for Western consumers (McCartney 2005), has become much more accessible for all. Although the internet has fundamentally shifted how we consume (a point to be returned to shortly) the offline physical consumption of counterfeit goods remains important.

Given the huge growth in the travel and tourism market, stimulated by low cost airlines and access to credit, it is not unsurprising there remains a concern about the relationship between people going on holiday and counterfeit consumption. Various market research surveys suggest a significant proportion of holiday makers buy counterfeits abroad. For example, Kelkoo (an online shopping and price comparison site) suggested that 45 percent of UK holiday makers travelling abroad in 2010 bought counterfeit fashion items. They further suggested that the opportunity to buy counterfeits was, for many holidaymakers, a driver in where they travelled (see The Herald 2011; Eyeflare 2013). Existing research with consumers of counterfeit products (Ledbury Research 2006, 2007; Rutter and Bryce 2008) cites availability of counterfeits abroad as an important factor in consumption. The data collected in this research supported this, highlighting holidays and overseas travel as important. This was both for knowing and unknowing buyers of counterfeit fashion. China, notorious for its prevalence in the global supply of counterfeit goods (see Lin 2011), and South East Asian countries cropped up frequently in accounts of counterfeit consumption, as did places like Italy, Greece, Spain and Turkey. Olivia, a 27 year old postgraduate student, described:

> I've only bought a few fashion fakes that I am aware of. I bought a coat in Thailand and a few tops and things. I didn't take many clothes out to Thailand, so I needed them and I didn't really care if they were fake since all these types of clothes are made in places like Thailand anyway. I think 'what's the difference'?   (Olivia)

The availability and seeming openly ease of buying counterfeit goods abroad may also mean that it is easier for consumers to unintentionally buy counterfeit fashion. Charlie (29 year old male employed full time as a labourer who described that he would only buy branded fashion goods and spent a lot of money on designer products), was one of the consumers who held the most negative views towards counterfeit goods and described how he had unknowingly bought counterfeit fashion items on a number of occasions on holiday. Charlie only later realised the items were not genuine and suggested that the alcohol he consumed on holiday might well have contributed to this happening.

> I bought a watch once; that was on holiday in Turkey. When I got back, I must have had too much to drink on holiday; the watch said Tommy Hifiger instead of Hilfiger.   (Charlie)

Even as consumption habits change and evolve, particularly with the movement towards online shopping, increased global travel suggests that this will remain an important way in which people consume counterfeit fashion. This appeared to be at least partly related to the uncertainty consumers had about the legal status of purchasing counterfeit goods. Although the purchase of counterfeit goods is not necessarily an illegal behaviour, many consumers are unclear about what does and does not constitute breaking the law when it comes to counterfeit goods. Even when consumers believe that buying a counterfeit is not breaking the law they often still considered it as illicit (Cordell et al. 1996). This is likely to be exacerbated by attempts from industry groups and regulatory authorities to make counterfeits 'socially stigma[tised]' (Mackenzie 2010: 132; see also Large 2015). The highly opportunistic nature of much 'holiday' consumption due to its ease and availability which was important for many consumers appeared to also be caught up in [mis]understandings of legal status and concerns about ethical behaviour and are highlighted in the accounts by Olivia (27 year old female) and Alfie (38 year old male) below:

Alfie: I would be aware of the legality of buying fakes in the UK, but overseas in China where it is so culturally embedded it didn't seem much of an issue.

Interviewer: Do you think that you would have bought it over here?

Alfie: Maybe not, no. I'd guess there'd be a bit of snobbery about.
                    I've only rarely bought fakes, like when I've been on holiday, and when you are on holiday you forget a bit about your morals and things like that. (Olivia)

Traditional criminological explanations such as that of routine activities theory may seem useful to explain counterfeit consumption here. Felson (1998: 68) argues that the following are needed for a deviant 'vice' (or transaction) to take place: firstly the setting needs to be favourable (combination of counterfeits being available and consumer being abroad), secondly their needs to be an 'absence of a place manager' (no 'capable guardian' who would interfere with the transaction) and finally, some form of 'camouflage' (even something such as a crowd, or potentially just by being abroad). However, it is also possible that being abroad, as well as an increased availability (or at least ease of access to counterfeits) acts as a dis-inhibitor where people might act in a way in which they would usually not at 'home'. This could be on the one hand purchasing fashion goods which one would not normally buy, or on the other taking risks which one would not normally take. One explanation for this could lie with 'moral holidays' (Presdee 2000: 64). In the 'consumption of crime' (although in this sense counterfeits rather than violence) the ability of a holiday seems to enable the displacement of an individual's morals and concerns about what is legal (or quasi legal, see Cordell et al. 1996). McCartney's (2005: 84) account of counterfeiting suggested 'people who would never dream of breaking the law at home seemed to forget that other countries' laws also count as illegal'. McCartney, and also Vagg (1995), attribute the desire of counterfeits when abroad to in the past when counterfeits were a symbol of the 'exotic' – when there was not as much overseas travel and therefore a counterfeit was 'exclusive in its own way'. They were cheap but 'not everyone could have them' (McCartney 2005: 85). These kinds of explanations however simply reinforce the notion of counterfeit consumption as deviant and fail to stand up in contemporary accounts of globalised leisure.

Ease of availability was fundamental for many purchases with several consumers describing how they bought fakes they came across on market stalls because they were both cheap and readily available. In some cases, this was clearly not about trying to buy a replica of a brand they knew. Erin (46 year old female who works part time in a shop) described a fake she bought which although she assumed was a counterfeit, did not actually recognise the brand. For Erin, what was more important than the brand was that she 'liked' the product and its "cheap price". As hinted at previously, a clear thread running through all the research with consumers regarding their counterfeit purchasing behaviour, intentions and attitudes was that attempting to simplify their motivations for purchasing a product down to one sole factor is misleading and underestimates the complexity of consuming counterfeit fashion. Poppy's (19 year old, works full time but lives at home described herself as very fashion conscious and spent a considerable portion of her disposable income on apparel and accessories) account of a holiday counterfeit purchase highlights the muddled process of consuming:

> When I was on holiday with my mum, I bought a Prada bag, just a black one, but again that was more because I liked it; I hate Prada! Actually, that's a lie: I went looking for a Chanel bag. I wanted the style; I don't like to flash labels. (Poppy)

Poppy, as did others, suggested that they buy counterfeits because they firstly like the product, but also in some sense are drawn to the brand – as in Poppy's case, this may not be to the overt labelling of the brand, but may be more about the style which is associated with that brand. Here we see problems in adopting a narrow definition of counterfeiting being strictly about trademarks – design piracy issues are also important. Oliver recognises that although he did like the style of the product, he was also interested in the brand of the product:

> I bought some fake sunglasses although on holiday and I quite liked the style. I was drawn to them because they were fakes and looked quite convincing. However, I think I liked the style of them and if it hadn't of been a copy then I probably would have bought them anyway. (Oliver)

To suggest all counterfeit consumption abroad is only about opportunity and ease of access ignores those who actively seek out products. Phillips (2005) described airline cabin crew taking orders from family and friends to bring back desired counterfeits on their travels. This notion, albeit in a different context, was described by Amy, the fashion and design student:

> The place where I used to work was based in China, and a lot of people who worked there would often go out to China and bring things back for friends and stuff. You could just send a picture of what you want and in China you can buy it anywhere and have it sent back. (Amy)

Buying Counterfeits Online

The internet and associated developments in technologies have fundamentally changed how we consume. Not only do we now have 24-hour access to a huge range of products, producers and retailers – both licit and illicit – but with this a whole new dimension to consuming and consumption. Even over the past decade there have been major shifts and developments in how consumers use and interact with the internet and the evolving nature of technology means that this will continue to shift and change. As Crewe (2017: 143) notes, 'digitalization has revolutionized the way fashion is designed, produced and consumed'.

In the mid to latter 2000s buying fashion and clothes from the internet was less of the everyday occurrence it has become a decade or so later: although buying products online was becoming the norm, many consumers reported that when it came to fashion they preferred to physically go shopping on the high street and tended to use the internet more occasionally. In addition, where we buy from online has changed in this period. For example, in the mid-2000s, eBay was one of the 'most visited shopping site[s] on the internet' (Alexa 2006 cited in Dengri-Knott and Molesworth 2010: 62) and was also considered a primary site for counterfeit sales. Ethnographic research on counterfeit sellers by Treadwell (2012) highlighted the importance of eBay for supply. Many consumers also described how they had (knowingly and unknowingly) previously bought counterfeit fashion from eBay. One consumer described a scenario where they bought an item thinking it was genuine and only realising it must be fake when it arrived and subsequently broke. The issue of consumers being deceived is hardly surprising given the tactics used by sellers such as that of "Des" in Treadwell's study:

> What I do is I get a good photograph of an authentic bag that is the copy of the one you are selling. Nowadays, you can take a few photos in a shop on

your mobile, go into Selfridges and that, easy. It makes it look even more real, fucking sneaky eh, and then I'll use that to sell fakes and they [eBay] don't delete your listings. ('Des' counterfeit seller cited in Treadwell 2012: 182)

Unlike being able to physically have a look at the item as you would in a shop, or even at a market stall, the consumer relies on an honest and accurate description of the product when buying online. Although websites such as eBay have been pressured to introduce protections for consumers and brands to guard against counterfeit products being sold and may well respond to take down requests if a fake item is spotted for sale, the proliferation of marketplace style websites and consumer to consumer selling platforms causes huge problems in the regulation of selling counterfeit fashion – as it does for the sale of goods more generally. As we see the range of platforms that enable the sale of goods continue to evolve and expand it is both easier for consumers to seek out counterfeit goods, and for sellers to distribute them (see Action Fraud 2018 and NTSeCT 2018 for an overview of these kinds of issues). Further, counterfeit goods proliferate on sites that are not really about selling. Social media platforms such as Instagram (based on posting images) have become a popular means of advertising, selling and buying counterfeit fashion (see Stroppa et al. 2016; Brandbastion 2018; Zerbo 2018).

Both the surface web and the dark web have provided huge expansions to how we can consume, how we choose to consume, and how consumers can be misled in their consumption. Technological developments do however cause significant problems for individual choice-based explanations of consumption – counterfeit or otherwise. Markets, trends and fashion now exist far beyond geographical boundaries (Crewe 2017) and the nature of algorithms and sponsored adverts changes what we see online (see Beer 2017). Increasingly sophisticated 'smart machines', that previously may have been reliant on a consumer initiating an automated process (knowingly or unknowingly), are now 'initiating and even controlling' consumption – or as Ritzer describes – prosumption (Ritzer 2014: 413).

THE PROBLEM WITH AUTHENTICITY

Shifts in technology and how we consume cause problems not only for consumers in distinguishing the likelihood of a product being counterfeit or genuine, but, further contribute to the blurring of notions of authenticity. As outlined in Chap. 1, distinctions between 'knowing' and 'unknowing' consumers of counterfeit fashion are problematic if treated as binary. When it comes to fashion, other than perhaps from an economic impact perspective, it is further questionable whether it is even that much of a useful way to conceptualise counterfeit consumption. The following account from Jack (32 year old male who is full time employed spending on average £200 –£300 a month on apparel/accessories) highlights that although he claimed not to knowingly buy counterfeits, this may not be strictly the truth:

Jack: I've bought some red Prada shoes, yeah, I've bought quite a few things … I wouldn't have bought anything really if I thought it was a fake, but would I buy just because [it's] a fake? No, I buy things on eBay I know are cheap.
Interviewer: So, would you rely on eBay to say if it is fake or genuine?
Jack: I buy things that say they are 100% genuine then I will buy, I would never buy anything if it said it was fake on eBay.
Interviewer: Even if you knew they were actually fake?
Jack: Well I didn't know, the only thing that suggested that they might be was the cost. So that is the thing, on some things I have bought they have looked fake and I don't wear these as much, and some things I have bought, although I have not done for a long time, I don't tend to use the computer as much and that is probably why. Some things I can't tell and for me, those are just a fantastic deal.
Jack: So really, it's just about price why I bought them, if they [red Prada shoes] had been fake then I would have been disappointed, I think. Would I stop wearing them? Err, if you couldn't find a difference then no. Because for me, they would be real.
Interviewer   So as long as they pass as real you are quite happy to wear fakes?
Jack: Yes, yes. Absolutely.

The symbolic value of buying into a brand, for some, may be more important than whether the product was actually produced by that brand. Throughout the research it was clear that conceptions about authenticity of a product were very much blurred for consumers. This might have been associated with where they were purchased, or, a lack of understanding about the legitimacy of a product. Buying a product abroad or online appeared to mitigate a consumers' ability, or desire, to establish whether a product was genuine. Counterfeit selling techniques often play on this: it is not uncommon to see products sold as "genuine fakes". As consumption increases through non-traditional channels like social media – where key word hashtag searches and sponsored adverts play an important role, combined with images positioning products on 'micro celebrities' or other 'influencers' products can take on different meanings and appearances with fluidity. This calls into question when does a product go from being genuine to fake? Temporal, cultural and spatial contexts will feed into this conundrum. It is also evident that consumers do not just buy counterfeit versions that have a genuine alternative, proving further problems for the idea that every counterfeit equates to a "lost sale". Counterfeit products may be available in different colours, designs and styles to those that are for sale legitimately and appear to fulfil a different purpose than those that exactly replicate an existing product.

Additionally, there are problems in seeing consumers and sellers as two distinct groups. There are clearly consumers who buy, wear and sell counterfeits in addition to those who buy solely for selling, or those who just buy for personal use. Antonopoulos et al. (2018) describe sellers who save up to buy a supply of counterfeit products when on holiday to bring back to sell. The internet further changes dynamics of demand and supply. Platforms such as Facebook Marketplace and Instagram provide easy opportunities for a wide range of sellers to engage in counterfeit supply: from small scale to large scale.

'Vulnerable', 'Hoodwinked' and Non-counterfeit Consumers

There is a tendency to position non-counterfeit consumers and counterfeit consumers as fundamentally different, and further, to separate counterfeit consumers into those who knowingly buy counterfeits against those who are deceived into buying counterfeits. Although differentiating non-counterfeit consumers as characteristically different (either in terms of their demographics or fashion preferences) seems largely unhelpful, recognising differences in counterfeit consumption does appear to be the most useful way to loosely generalise consumers. However, there must be recognition that there is a considerable amount of fluidity and overlap between these groups. More importantly, within these groups people's reasons for engaging – or not engaging – with counterfeits differ, so they will only ever offer a starting point. As we can see above with perceptions of legality abroad, even at an individual level, perceptions of acceptability and legality are spatially, temporally and culturally dependent (see Hudson 2019). Further, within these groups, consumers' preferences for fashion, will also vary. Of course, one of the biggest drawbacks in any kind of assessment of counterfeit consumption, is the reliance on the consumer to have recognised – or admit – a product is counterfeit.

Here I suggest three broad groups. First, are the group of consumers who have never bought a counterfeit and do not intend too. This might be due to holding views about counterfeiting as harmful or otherwise culturally negative, or, due to fashion consumption preferences. The second group are the deceived – or at the least – unsure at time of purchase consumers, or as Rojek (2017) describes: the 'hoodwinked'. However, assuming all consumers in this group are *concerned* about their purchase being counterfeit is inaccurate. For some such as Charlie and Daisy, this was very much the case – for others such as James, this was not so. The third group knowingly have and/or knowingly would, is useful to break down into further subgroups: those who have bought a counterfeit and those who would – albeit not necessarily have done so previously; and those who have previously bought a counterfeit but would *not* do so again.

The Counterfeit Consumer Myth

This chapter set out to explore the consumption of counterfeit fashion goods through investigating popular ideas about counterfeit consumption and consumers. The situation and context of counterfeit consumption is important, especially for more opportunistic buyers. This may be as it is simply easier to access counterfeit goods; because in different contexts we might be less concerned about a goods authenticity or perhaps because in certain contexts we are less likely to be able to recognise the cues and indicators that might suggest something is counterfeit.

Although inevitably cost is an important factor in the decision to buy a counterfeit the nature of something being cheap is subjective. Further, the growth of disposable fashion and value retailing suggests that consumers do not necessarily equate something being cheap as poor quality, or undesirable. Importantly there appears little support for the idea that counterfeit consumers are typically young and from low income backgrounds.

Counterfeit consumption takes place across a broad range of consumers of different ages, backgrounds and occupations.

The situation and context of counterfeit consumption for some consumers was very important. For example, some consumers described that they would buy counterfeits although abroad but this was not something they would do in the UK. This primarily appeared to be about the ease of access and availability of counterfeits in certain destinations. This was particularly the case when consumers visited countries where the genuine items were produced or where counterfeiting was so rife it was considered difficult to buy something genuine. On the one hand, for some consumers it was more difficult to recognise the cues that might indicate something is counterfeit, and, on the other hand, there appeared to be less of a concern about a goods authenticity. The heightened level of counterfeit consumption particularly for consumers on holiday also reflected 'going shopping' as a key leisure practice for tourists. The increase in global travel and emphasis on travel as a primary leisure activity may well be a factor in the popularity of counterfeit fashion consumption.

The increasingly globalised consumer and evolving nature of technology also reflects shifts in consumption of fashion online. Although initially many consumers appeared reluctant to purchase fashion goods from the internet (unless it was something they were buying from a store they were familiar with), how we consume has shifted dramatically and we now see more outlets and modes than ever to shop. The whole concept of shopping as a leisure activity has changed as we now live in an era where we can purchase goods with ease from an app on our mobile phone. There are also increasingly blurred lines between the producer (retailer) and consumer with it now easier than ever for consumer to consumer selling. In terms of counterfeits it is easier than ever for those selling counterfeits to infiltrate legitimate supply chains and harder for consumers to recognise counterfeits: existing cues about quality, price or website are often meaningless in these new retail environments. At the same time, it is easier than ever for consumers to seek out counterfeits: automated advertising through algorithms will further ensure this process. In terms of the role of situation and context, the internet can be suggested to play a similar role to being abroad: a greater willingness to engage in what might be considered 'risky' behaviour, or, simply open-up more opportunities for consumption.

In conclusion, although cost, location and other superficial factors are important to an extent in counterfeit consumption, this only goes part of the way to explain consumption and explain why people consume counterfeit fashion. Chapter 3 will take on these ideas and explore further the motivations and micro dynamics of consumer behaviour within a broader context of the consumption of 'legal' and legitimate fashion goods.

REFERENCES

ACG. (2003). *What Do Consumers Really Think About Fakes? Section 1.* Anti Counterfeiting Group. Available from: www.a-cg.com. Accessed 01 Sept 2007.

Action Fraud. (2018). *Counterfeit Goods Fraud.* Available from: https://www.actionfraud.police.uk/fraud_protection/counterfeit_goods. Accessed 22 July 2018.

Antonopoulos, G. A., Hall, A., Large, J., Shen, A., Crang, M., & Andrews, M. (2018). *Fake Goods, Real Money. The Counterfeiting Business and Its Financial Management.* Bristol: Policy Press.

Archer, L., Hollingworth, S., & Halsall, A. (2007). University's Not for Me – I'm a Nike Person: Urban, Working-Class Young People's Negotiations of 'Style', Identity and Educational Engagement. *Sociology, 41*(2), 219–237.

BASCAP (Business Action to Stop Counterfeiting and Piracy). (2009). *Research Report on Consumer Attitudes and Perceptions of Counterfeiting and Piracy.* Available from: http://www.iccwbo.org/uploadedFiles/BASCAP/Pages/BASCAP-Consumer%20Research%20Report_Final.pdf. Accessed 21 Aug 2011.

Beer, D. (2017). The Social Power of Algorithms. *Information, Communication and Society, 20*(1), 1–13.

Bloch, P. H., Bush, R. F., & Campbell, L. (1993). "Consumer Accomplices" in Product Counterfeiting: A Demand Side Investigation. *The Journal of Consumer Marketing, 10*(4), 27–36.

Bothwell, C. (2005). Burberry Versus the Chavs. *BBC News Online.* Available from: http://news.bbc.co.uk/1/hi/business/4381140.stm. Accessed 04 May 2011.

Brandbastion. (2018). *How Counterfeit Sellers Are Hijacking Luxury Brands on Instagram.* Brandbastion. Available from: https://blog.brandbastion.com/how-counterfeit-goods-are-hijacking-luxury-brands-on-instagram. Accessed 22 July 2018.

Cordell, V. W., Wongtada, N., & Kieschnick, R. L. (1996). Counterfeit Purchase Intentions: Role of Lawfulness, Attitudes and Product Traits as Determinants. *Journal of Business Research, 35*, 41–53.

Crewe, L. (2017). *The Geographies of Fashion. Consumption, Space and Value.* London: Bloomsbury.

Dengri-Knott, J., & Molesworth, M. (2010). Love It. Buy It. Sell It. Consumer Desire and the Social Drama of eBay. *Journal of Consumer Culture, 10*(1), 56–79.

Douglas, M., & Isherwood, B. ([1979] 1996). *The World of Goods. Towards an Anthropology of Consumption*. London: Routledge.

Eyeflare. (2013). *Travellers Bring Back 0.5 Billion Pounds Worth of Fake Goods Every Year*. Eyeflare Travel Advice and Tips. Available from: https://www.eyeflare.com/article/travellers-buy-half-billion-worth-fake-goods-every-year/. Accessed 02 Jan 2018.

Felson, M. (1998). *Crime and Everyday Life* (2nd ed.). Thousand Oaks: Pine Forge Press.

Hall, S., Winlow, S., & Ancrum, C. (2008). *Criminal Identities and Consumer Culture. Crime, Exclusion and the New Culture of Narcissism*. Devon: Willan.

Hayward, K. J. (2004). *City Limits: Crime, Consumer Culture and the Urban Experience*. London: The Glasshouse Press.

Hayward, K., & Yar, M. (2006). The 'Chav' Phenomenon: Consumption, Media and the Construction of a New Underclass. *Crime, Media, Culture, 2*(1), 9–28.

Hudson, R. (2019). Economic Geographies of the (il)legal and the (il)licit. In T. Hall & V. Scalia (Eds.), *A Research Agenda in Global Crime*. London: Edward Elgar.

IPO. (2016). *Protecting Creativity, Supporting Innovation: IP Enforcement 2020*. Newport: Intellectual Property Office. Available from: https://www.gov.uk/government/uploads/system/uploads/attachment_data/file/571604/IP_Enforcement_Strategy.pdf. Accessed 16 Dec 2017.

Jones, O. (2011). *Chavs. The Demonisation of the Working Class*. London: Verso.

Large, J. (2015). "Get Real Don't Buy Fakes". Fashion Fakes and Flawed Policy: The Problem with Taking a Consumer – Responsibility Approach to Reducing the Problem of Counterfeiting. *Criminology and Criminal Justice, 15*(2), 169–185.

Ledbury Research. (2006). *Counterfeiting Luxury: Exposing the Myths*. Davenport Lyons. Available from: www.a-cg.com. Accessed 22 Sept 2010.

Ledbury Research. (2007). *Counterfeiting Luxury: Exposing the Myths*. 2nd edition. Davenport Lyons. Available from: www.a-cg.com. Accessed 22 Sept 2010.

Lin, Y. J. (2011). *China and the Rise of Counterfeit Goods*. London: Routledge.

Mackenzie, S. (2010). Fakes. In F. Brookman, M. Maguire, H. Pierpoint, & T. Bennett (Eds.), *Handbook on Crime*. Devon: Willan.

McCartney, S. (2005). *The Fake Factor: Why We Love Brands But Buy Fakes*. London: Cyan.

Morgan, L. R., & Birtwistle, G. (2009). An Investigation of Young Fashion Consumers' Disposable Habits. *International Journal of Consumer Studies, 33*, 190–198.

NSeCT. (2018). *Who Are the National Trading Standards eCrime Team*. Available from: http://www.tradingstandardsecrime.org.uk/about-us/. Accessed 22 July 2018.

OECD. (2007). *The Economic Impact of Counterfeiting*. Executive Summary. Organisation for Economic Co-operation and Development. Available from: https://www.oecd.org/sti/38707619.pdf. Accessed 04 Jan 2018.

Phillips, T. (2005). *Knockoff. The Deadly Trade in Counterfeit Goods*. London: Kogan Page.

Presdee, M. (2000). *Cultural Criminology and the Carnival of Crime*. London: Routledge.

Ritzer, G. (2014). Automating Prosumption. The Decline of the Prosumer and the Rise of the Prosuming Machines. *Journal of Consumer Culture, 15*(3), 407–424.

Rojek, C. (2017). Counterfeit Commerce; Relations of Production, Distribution and Exchange. *Cultural Sociology, 11*(1), 28–43.

Rutter, J., & Bryce, J. (2008). The Consumption of Counterfeit Goods. "Here Be Pirates". *Sociology, 42*(6), 1146–1164.

Solomon, M. R., & Rabolt, N. J. (2004). *Consumer Behaviour in Fashion*. New Jersey: Prentice Hall.

Stroppa, A., di Stefano, D., & Parrella, B. (2016). Social Media and Luxury Goods Counterfeit: A Growing Concern for Government, Industry and Consumers Worldwide. *The Washington Post*. Available from: https://www.washington-post.com/blogs/the-switch/files/2016/05/IG_A2016_ST2.pdf?noredirect=on. Accessed 22 July 2018.

The Herald. (2011, July 21). Half of Tourists Buy Counterfeit Goods. *The Herald*. Available from: http://www.pressreader.com/uk/the-herald/20110721/281882999999116. Accessed 02 Jan 2018.

Tom, G., Garibaldi, B., Zeng, Y., & Pilcher, J. (1998). Consumer Demand for Counterfeit Goods. *Psychology and Marketing, 15*(5), 405–421.

Treadwell, J. (2012). From the Car Boot to Booting It Up? eBay, Online Counterfeit Crime and the Transformation of the Criminal Marketplace. *Criminology and Criminal Justice, 12*(2), 175–192.

Vagg, J. (1995). The Policing of Signs: Trademark Infringement and Law Enforcement. *European Journal on Criminal Policy and Research, 3*(2), 75–91.

Yurchisin, J., & Johnson, K. K. P. (2010). *Fashion and the Consumer*. Oxford: Berg.

Zerba, J. (2018, February 7). The Weird Economy of Instagram Fashion Knock Offs. *Dazed*. Available from: http://www.dazeddigital.com/fashion/article/38922/1/the-weird-economy-of-instagram-fashion-knock-offs-counterfeit-items-china. Accessed 22 July 2018.

CHAPTER 3

Consuming Fakes, Consuming Fashion

Abstract This chapter explores why people buy counterfeit fashion through examining the dynamics of consumer purchasing behaviour and attitudes towards the consumption of counterfeit fashion. This chapter argues that although cost, location and other superficial factors are important to an extent, this only goes part of the way to explain consumption. The main thrust of the argument centres on motivations for consuming counterfeit goods needing to be contextualised within an understanding about consumption of legitimate fashion goods. This is largely due to the nature of the fashion process being one of 'introduction and imitation'. Not only is the industry based on a continual perpetuation of consumer desire for new products but the very nature of fashion and the sustainability of consumer industries, is inherently based on copying.

Keywords Consuming counterfeits • Fashion industry • Consumption • Copying & imitation

INTRODUCTION

Generalising a counterfeit buyer in terms of their typical demographic characteristics, 'deviant' values or lack of moral integrity is problematic and fails to offer much by way of a useful explanation for counterfeit fashion consumption. In common with this, over-emphasising factors such as

© The Author(s) 2019
J. Large, *The Consumption of Counterfeit Fashion*, Palgrave Studies in Risk, Crime and Society,
https://doi.org/10.1007/978-3-030-01331-8_3

a counterfeit's cost or where they are being sold, adds little to explaining counterfeit fashion consumption beyond surface-level purchase explanations. Chapter 2 explored how some consumers buy counterfeits for what they are ('I like the product') and how cost and availability may impact on the propensity to buy a counterfeit. However, this does not go far enough to understand the desire for fashion products in the first place, or the contemporary nature of consumption. Therefore, it appears a different exploration of the consumption of counterfeit fashion is needed which contextualises this within broader motivations for consuming fashion. This chapter will adopt the position that motivations for consuming counterfeit fashion should be understood within an understanding of motivations for consuming fashion more generally. Why is it that we consume fashion products and how does this relate to counterfeit fashion consumption?

Taking first the discussion around trademarks, branded 'designer' goods and fashion preferences this chapter examines the desirability of these items and their consumption. Within this discussion I examine how brands signal factors such as quality and fit to consumers and explore how this relates to notions of social desirability. The chapter continues with attempting to drill down into understanding why consumers buy some fashion items and not others. Here the chapter examines the role of the fashion cycle and industry in terms of shaping what is 'fashionable' and how what we wear relates to perceptions of style and identity. This reflects on theoretical understandings that situate fashion as a means of consumer choice to construct identity versus how the fashion industry shapes and controls consumer 'choice'. Against the backdrop of these discussions this chapter then considers how this relates to the consumption of counterfeit fashion. Building on these discussions, the final section of this chapter explores the emotional nature of fashion and consumption and how it makes us *feel*. This highlights the feelings of pleasure and gratification against the exacerbating of our insecurities and anxieties. Reflecting on earlier discussions around understandings of fashion and counterfeit fashion consumption, here I question the over-emphasis on 'rational' consumption. Finally, through reflecting back on the importance of fashion in contemporary consumption this chapter will finish by examining how the very nature of fashion can be argued to legitimise and promote the consumption of counterfeit fashion goods.

THE CONSUMPTION OF FASHION

Once getting beyond surface-level decisions related to price and the routes to access counterfeits, consumer preferences around counterfeit goods are tied into constructions and interactions around fashion consumption. Views on fashion brands, habits of consumption and how these interact with attitudes towards counterfeiting seem to take on much more significance. Although nearly everyone engages with buying fashion goods to some extent (in the broadest sense i.e. including non-branded goods, high street clothing etc. as well as luxury, branded and sports clothing), this ranges from those who buy clothing for functional reasons, to those who are highly conscious of fashion and place considerable emphasis on what they wear, how they look and so on. People also shop for fashion items with differing frequency – some shop for fashion items on a regular, even daily basis, others much more occasionally. At the same time, shopping does not just have to be about buying, as often going shopping does not result in a purchase – yet as the intention might not have been to buy something, the shopping event may still be viewed as a success (Shaw 2010: 2). Many consumers take satisfaction and enjoyment out of 'browsing'; reflecting the role of shopping as a primary example of contemporary leisure.

Although characteristics of products such as their price, their quality or the brand name may be important at an individual level, broader influences from the fashion industry, media and everyday experiences also impact on the consumption of fashion. Elements of consumption may take place in a process which can be understood by consumer decision making models, but in practice, much consumption of fashion is impulsive and unplanned. For many consumers, although they might set out to buy something specific, their shopping event would result in several other purchases. Yurchisin and Johnson (2010: 75) highlight the differences between Solomon and Rabolt's (2004: 447) definition of 'unplanned buying' where 'we are 'prompted to buy something while in the store' that we did not plan to buy before we entered' and Rook's (1987: 191) definition of 'impulse buying' where 'you feel 'a sudden', often powerful and persistent urge to buy something immediately' without 'regard for its consequences'. Many people buy fashion goods without really thinking about it, as Chloe (24 year old in full time employment – described herself as fashion conscious and although previously had bought counterfeits now held strong views against intellectual property rights infringement more generally) said: "I don't know why I buy half of what I buy". The very nature of the fashion industry is reliant on this for its sustained economic success and thus promotes and perpetuates a continual cycle of consumption.

Traditional economic theory, which is fundamentally assumed in most understandings of counterfeit demand (see Chap. 2) suggests that people buy goods in a rational manner being conscious of price. Yet, asking people about their consumption habits challenges the idea of a rationally minded, price conscious consumer. Economic theories themselves have thus moved away from such ideas and recognise that people may consume goods for other reasons (Belk 1995). At the same time despite the impulsive and/or unplanned nature of much buying of fashion goods which was apparent within the research, most consumers do not have the financial ability to buy everything that they want, and therefore there must be some element of a decision-making process with an economic focus (Yurchisin and Johnson 2010). This suggests that price and quality as factors are important; and a brand name can also act as a 'heuristic' to help a consumer make a 'speedy decision' (Solomon and Rabolt 2004: 367).

As explored previously, there appears to be little value in distinguishing counterfeit consumers and non-counterfeit consumers in terms of their demographic characteristics. What does, however, seem to play more relevance is the consumer's engagement with fashion. This was not as simple as those who buy branded goods versus those who do not – nor – those who attempt to be 'fashion conscious' versus those who take a more 'functional' approach. Counterfeit fashion consumption spanned these different consumer types. Although in some cases, it is possible to draw a parallel with more standardised counterfeit consumption explanations, the narratives told by consumers of their counterfeiting shopping experiences and preferences, played into their wider fashion consumption. The remainder of this chapter will explore this issue in more detail.

Joshua, Charlie and Jack were explicit about the brand being the reason for purchasing an item. Joshua, a 20 year old student who spent an average of £200–£300 a month on apparel and accessories was very much against counterfeiting. Charlie, a 29 year old labourer, also spent similar amounts on fashion goods and like Joshua, was against counterfeiting. However, Charlie had realised that on a number of occasions, he had been deceived into buying counterfeit goods. Jack aged 32 and employed as a university academic, although spending similar amounts in terms of monthly average on fashion to Joshua and Charlie, had more complex views on the acceptability of counterfeits. For Jack, it was important that he considered the product 'real' at the time of purchase – discovering a product was (or potentially was) counterfeit at a subsequent point in time was less problematic for Jack than knowingly buy a counterfeit product. All three however strongly identified with branded and designer fashion and considered themselves as 'fashion conscious' consumers. For Joshua, brand names represented quality, and justified his spending and his rationale for not buying fakes.

Joshua: If you pay £50 for a shirt then £10 for a fake then already that tells me that the fitting is going to be nicer and the quality as well. You could put something through the wash that is fake, and it would shrink.

Interviewer: So, you spend more, the better value you get for your money?

Joshua: Yeah.

Daisy (20 year old start-up fashion designer, cautious about the damaging nature of disposable fashion, large fashion companies and mass consumption) recognised that because she is becoming more concerned about good quality products this has resulted in her being less concerned about price. For Daisy, quality related more to independent and smaller brands, than the kinds of brands Jack, Charlie and Joshua favoured. Being able to associate with particular brands however did clearly signify product quality for these consumers. Jack described how certain designer labels were preferable due to their representation of product quality.

> I like to buy things – you know for instance, this was an impulse buy [shows jacket]. I like to buy things that I know are going to last, which won't go out of fashion and which are valuable, and which are of quality and look understated.   (Jack)

As Jack indicates, buying branded goods is not just about what the brand represents in terms of perceived product quality. Charlie was emphatic that he would not wear a product if it did not show a recognised brand name:

> It's got to have a name on it. If it ain't got a name on it, then I won't buy it.   (Charlie)

Ruby (21 year old student) also showed what brands can mean to consumers:

Interviewer: Do you think that you would have bought that bag if it was just a generic bag and not a brand?
Ruby: Probably not. The brand was the reason for actually liking it.

Charlie and Ruby represent what we more typically think of when we consider the consumption of well-known branded fashion products; where the signifier of the label may be the most important factor of a product. For some consumers who have a close interest or affinity with a brand or designer, buying branded goods is not about buying labels simply because they are labels, but because of associating with the 'story' of the brand – of course this is one of the primary marketing strategies brands invest in. Brands are about much more than selling a product – they represent a symbol, a lifestyle, an image (Klein 2000). Much like fashion is signified in different ways – whether it be 'a garment, a body, a shop, a catwalk, an idea, a photograph, a memory, a moving image on screen…' (Crewe 2017: 136), brands seek to entice the consumer into their 'story' through a product. This appeal of luxury brands is outlined by Amy, a 22 year old fashion and design student.

Interviewer: what makes you want to buy into a certain designer?
Amy: Well, Alexander McQueen is one of the big ones. One of the girls here got a scarf this week, just in sort of memory of him. There's a lot of other things that go on like with the films, like when Chanel first came out I think it increases your knowledge about them [the brands]. I think it's just with the clothes that you like. Because when you study it constantly you look at the catwalks, after four years of it you tend to know what you like best. So, year on year if you like that type of brand you're going to go for that brand.
Interviewer: So, the more you know about the brand, it increases your desire for it?
Amy: The more I know about it the more of a personality the clothes have. Rather than just buying a Prada label or Gucci label, we know what's behind that label.

Inevitably, there is a logical parallel that consumers who seek out branded goods are the most likely to come across counterfeit goods. For Amy, counterfeits provided a way of being able to engage with a brand she could not otherwise afford.

Amy:	I don't really care that it's [handbag] fake. We [fashion students] understand that we give enough money to the brands, and we study them. I think a lot of the things that we want are more expensive that what we can afford so we often tend to buy [counterfeit] things because we can't afford to buy the real thing.
Interviewer:	So, is that the main reason you buy fakes because you can't afford them?
Amy:	But if I had the money I would definitely buy the original
Interviewer:	Is it important for you to buy luxury and designer goods because you are involved in fashion?
Amy:	More so only because we know the story behind it. And we've all learned all about 20th century fashion and how all the big designers made their mark. So, a lot of us have our favourite designers and we know their story, whereas a lot of people [who didn't study fashion] wouldn't know that bit. So, we want to buy into their story. However, we aren't giving them the money.
Interviewer:	So, you want to show that you're a part of the brand because you know about the history and the designer, but yet, you're happy to do so without buying into the actual proper brand?
Amy:	Yes, for now. It's only just until I can afford it.

Joshua and Charlie both explicitly only bought recognised designer or sportswear goods. Jack and Oliver (29 year old, full time employed) although also favouring branded goods both preferred 'luxury' branded goods. Joshua and Charlie were completely anti counterfeit products. Charlie had, however, been deceived into buying counterfeits on holiday. Oliver, although suggesting that his preferences were moving toward authentic, said that he was generally happy to engage with counterfeit goods, unless they were of one of specific brands that he was "loyal" to where described how it distressed him to see counterfeits of that brand. Jack again seemed to have mixed messages about counterfeits. Although

Jack had bought counterfeits in the past, he was keen to point out that although he later realised them to be counterfeit – and did not mind – it was important to him to buy items with the belief that they were real, however loose this belief was. For many consumers, associating with a brand in the sense of specific luxury or sports brand is not a priority but falls into a wider pattern of consumption of generic 'high street' goods. Lily (24 year old in full time employment who spends around £50–£100 a month on apparel/accessories and would not buy a counterfeit) described her mixed approach to buying branded and generic goods:

> Yeah, something nice and quirky, but it could be from Topshop, or something cheap from Primark, and then something nice from somewhere else. Mix and match.   (Lily)

Branded luxury and sportswear goods may have social desirability associated with the meaning and symbolism of the brand, yet the products themselves do not hold an innate desirability – this is informed, created and sold by the fashion industry. The extent to which consumers operate individual agency when consuming fashion is probably more problematic than most would like to admit. Fashion is sold to us as a way of expressing individuality and personality, yet, this is all part of the package. Although being out shopping, some consumers look for items that stand out to them and their preferences, a few of the interviewees (Chloe, Lily, Freya, Emily, Poppy and Daisy) talked about how they would often buy items which just happened to 'catch their eye' while they were looking around the shop. Of course, retailers recognise this, and shops are designed in such a way to encourage unplanned buying (Yurchisin and Johnson 2010). Unplanned, or impulsive buying, usually takes place with a 'rapid' decision and a 'subjective bias in favour of immediate possession' (Rook and Gardner 1993: 3).

Lily recognised although on a conscious level this attraction to certain items on view in shops might be related to her own personal preferences about what she liked, she also is probably influenced to some extent on a "subconscious level" by trends she had seen in magazines and on celebrities. For something to become fashionable it must be introduced and adopted, and magazines and celebrities provide a useful tool for fashion companies to do so. 'Fashion innovators' are those who first take up a new idea and others follow their fashion lead, therefore the high visibility nature of a popular celebrity, or the carefully manipulated photo-shoot of fashion models in a magazine provide an ideal way of introducing new styles, trends and items to the wider mass market (see Yurchisin and Johnson 2010; Crewe 2017 for a discussion). More recently, largely thanks to social media sites like Instagram and the rise of fashion bloggers, more informal marketing through fashion 'influencers' has taken hold (see Crewe 2017). Influences on trends and fashion now come in a multitude of directions. In addition to seeing things in magazines, on TV and online, people also see other people wearing things that they like on a more everyday basis and some participants would even go up to a stranger who they saw wearing an item and ask them where they got it from. However, others said that they did not have the confidence to do so and would go and look for something similar themselves.

> If I see something on the TV or on the street, I'll hunt something out whether it's that particular item or something similar I think 'Oh I like that look'.   (Oliver)

As technology develops and consuming fashion moves into unprecedented realms of digital sophistication and global reach (see Crewe 2017), searching out a look as described by Oliver, is increasingly less a needle in a haystack search, and when logging onto your smartphone, probably easily accessible via a couple of clicks thanks to automated adverts, algorithms, browser history's and web cookies (see Ritzer 2014; Beer 2017). Retailers and 'influencers' (whether they be TV stars, bloggers or 'celebrities') are increasingly teaming up to make a look – or product – easily and speedily accessible to the mass market of consumers. The 2018 series of *Love Island*, a British reality TV show which has gained huge viewing figures and credited for getting young people back to 'watching live TV' (Guardian 2018), saw contestants wearing clothes provided by certain retailers who then linked viewers directly to these products and looks via apps and sections on their websites dedicated specifically to achieving these looks, meaning viewers could shop for these looks and products as they watched each episode.

In addition to liking the look of something, the fit of a product is also important. This reflects the close relationship between fashion and the body. More than three quarters of the interview participants stated that fit was either the most important factor, or one of the most important factors, when buying a product. For some this meant a tendency to buy certain clothes from particular shops. The importance of fit and 'wearing the right clothes' enables people to 'feel at ease with [their] bodies'. Although fit is not the only element of wearing the 'right clothes', badly fitting clothes are likely to make people feel uncomfortable and potentially 'vulnerable' (Entwistle 2000: 7). Body concerns, whether it be age, weight or height impacted on consumers' engagement with fashion. Over a third of the interviewees talked clearly about how concerns about their body shape or age impacted on what they would or would not wear. For some, such as Millie, Lucy and Erin their primary concern was to dress in a way they felt appropriate for their age:

> I'm trying to do it so I don't look like mutton dressed as lamb. I'm quite conscious of what's fashionable for me rather than what's in fashion.
> (Millie, 41 year old fashion and design student)

> I'm more conscious because I'm older … but now I'm very conscious of my shape and making the most of it.   (Lucy, 56 year old employed by an independent clothing retailer)

> I like sort of a bit of fashion but because of my age, I'm 46, I wouldn't go to the extreme and they they'd think 'oh god she's really OTT for her age'. I tend to like fashion but take a bit of it and then do whatever I want with it.   (Erin, 46 year old, part time shop worker)

For others, their concern was to do with their body shape:

> I'm conscious of weight and I try to dress in a way which helps. (Harry, 28 year old male in full time employment)

> I'm conscious of my figure, so I have areas I want to accentuate and areas I want to hide. (Ella, 27 year old post graduate student)

These comments reinforce the work of Entwistle (2000: 35):

> Dress is the visible form of our intentions, but in everyday life dress is the insignia by which are read and come to read in others. Dress is part of the presentation of self; ideas of embarrassment and stigma play an important part in the experience of dress in everyday life and can be applied to discuss the ways in which dress has to 'manage' these as well as the way dress may sometimes be the source of our shame.

Although fashion is seen by many as a symbolic communicator reflecting individual choice, fashion is constrained by various structures and takes place within various temporal, spatial and cultural contexts (Sweetman 2001; Hayward 2004; Crewe 2017). Sweetman recognises wider social structures such as gender, age, ethnicity as well as dress code restrictions and policies which underpin and constrain individual choice. In addition to the sentiments regarding age above, body shape concerns were hugely important. Freya's (25 years old in full time employment for the health service) comments about how she was more conscious about dressing fashionably "now I've lost weight" really demonstrated this link. Fashion is regularly criticised for its use of 'stick thin' models on catwalks and the huge growth of the diet, fitness and beauty industry is closely associated with the fashion industry. Hesse-Biber (1996) describes the 'cult of thin-ness' of young women and discusses how this is perpetuated by society and industry. Interdisciplinary research by Grogan (2008) on body image found that media and popular portrayals of the attractive young, slender woman framed perceptions about body image,

> Many women cited pressure from the fashion industry to be slim saying that fashionable clothes only come in small sizes (British size 14 or below), so that to dress fashionably you have to be slim. (Grogan 2008: 52)

Perceptions of Style and Identity

Ultimately, regardless of how and why we explain it; consumers do consider what they wear in relation to how it makes them feel and the image they want to portray. Although the interview participants said that how they felt in themselves was most important, the majority also recognised that how they were perceived by others also mattered. Some had a clear idea of how they wanted to be seen by other people, and although a personal style was not always readily identifiable for some respondents, many cited a general concern with wanting to 'look good'. Joshua and Charlie wanted people to associate them with the brands that they were wearing. As Charlie said: "unless there's that [the brand name] then I don't feel comfortable". There is something about particular brand names which appeal to consumers such as Charlie and Joshua, who both only identify with popular designer and sports brand names (such as Armani, Stone Island, Ralph Lauren, Nike). Charlie described that although he did not want to look the same as anyone else who is engaging with similar brands in his peer group, he agreed that he wanted to be connected through wearing the same brands. Charlie described how he "feel[s] comfortable in brands I recognise". This is the whole point of branding – brands are selling consumers an image, a life-style, an identity – far more than just a product (Klein 2000).

For other consumers, their overall style was more important than association with a particular brand. Amelia described her very "formal" style, similar to Oliver who described his style as "smart". The three older female participants all described their style as "sophisticated" or "classic", and closely attributed their styles to their perceptions of how they *should* be dressing for their age. Others talked about wanting to be seen as "trendy" or "fashionable". Some participants positioned themselves as being different from the "mainstream" fashion industry using words like "quirky", "eclectic" and "alternative". For some, their biggest concern was about how their peers perceived them, whereas for others, although peer perception was important, they were also concerned about how they were perceived by others more generally. Notions of 'fitting in' and 'standing out' were also important.

> I just don't like to blend in. Just personal opinion really, I just like in a way to stand out … I don't know, I always feel that I like to stand out. Even the lacy top things, I'll get it, but I'll get something, like, I've got a pink baggier one rather than like the tight black ones everyone has got.   (Poppy, 19 years old, works full time in the service economy)

> I do have a particular look that people would associate with me. I like people to perceive me as smart and a bit individual. I'd maybe go for something that is a little bit unusual, whether it's unusual fabric or an unusual accessory or something. (Oliver, 29 years old working full time in professional services support)

Grace (29 years old, full time employed), who described her style as being quite "distinctive" described her dilemma of particular social situations where although wanting to keep her own style she does not "want to stand out too much". 'An individual may want to 'stand out' but she or he also wants to 'fit in' with a group' (Entwistle 2000: 139).

The Consumption of Counterfeit Fashion

Those who bought counterfeits tended to do so on an infrequent or sporadic basis rather than systematically. The situation and context of the counterfeit being sold may be important (see Chap. 2), yet, it is also evident that this alone does not sufficiently explain counterfeit consumption.

As with preferences for different types of products, perceptions of style and identity are important for consumers when it comes to engaging, or not, with counterfeits. On the one hand, there were the consumers who saw counterfeits as a positive way of reflecting their style. Amy as discussed above, bought counterfeits so that she was able to show her allegiance with her favourite brands. This was not at the expense of the sale of the genuine good. Amy saw nothing wrong with admitting she was wearing a counterfeit:

> As I'm studying fashion, I can normally recognise the brand and if it's fake or not. We normally mention if it was a fake, I would never hide the fact that I have a fake brand as a lot of us have real stuff too.   (Amy)

Grace who no longer buys branded goods authentic or counterfeit, discussed the value which counterfeits had when she was younger and at school:

> I wanted to blend in and be like everybody else. I wanted to be fashionable and have fashionable trainers for school. (Grace)

Grace's comments reflect findings by Archer et al. (2007: 227) who found that school pupils who wore "ugly trainers or cheap clothes" were bullied, taunted and ostracised and were positioned as "worthless". This suggests that for many young people, the need to commit themselves to their appearance (Archer et al. 2007) is essential. Research by Elliott and Leonard (2004) highlighted the importance for children wearing the correct brand of trainers to be popular and not to be viewed as poor. Therefore, it is possible to suggest that for those who have no other way of accessing the brand, a *good* counterfeit might be a better option than a cheap generic alternative.

Poppy and Erin were also quite happy to be seen wearing counterfeits and saw them as a means to engage with their broader interests in fashion. Alfie (38 year old post graduate student who spent on average less than £50 a month on fashion), who tended to steer away from branded goods more generally actually proposed that counterfeits could be a way of projecting his anti-brand identity:

Alfie: In some ways I'd be quite pleased [to tell people wearing counterfeit]. I'd be happy for people not to associate me with slavishly buying labels.

Interviewer: anti-fashion?
Alfie: Yeah, subverting it.

Positioning consumers such as Alfie, in terms of resistance, might seem like an obvious explanation and could satisfy explanations of why some consumers buy counterfeits. However, the tendency to position consumers as resisting cultural norms, or taking a stance against big business, is as problematic for explaining consuming counterfeits, as much as it is as an explanation more generally in criminology (see Hall and Winlow 2015). Given that branding and fashion relies on imitation, advertising and the communication of symbolic messages and desire, it is difficult to see how overall counterfeiting can have any real strength as the anti-fashion message described by Alfie. As Rojek (2017: 38) suggests

> The bulk of counterfeit trade is faithfully directed to supplying consumer demands for affordable prices and positive status differentiation. The positional judgements that consumers make in the counterfeit market may come with the frisson of risky business, but their net effect reproduces the price mechanism. Counterfeit commerce does not produce an alternative to the balance of surplus and scarcity in consumer relations. Luxury goods under copyright are still, on financial grounds, out of reach of the majority of consumers. Nor does the trade challenge the stigma of scarcity or the glamour of surplus. Only at the margins is the ironic consumption of counterfeit goods privileged over the certified value of commodities inscribed legally by copyright/patent.

These points made by Rojek can largely be seen in the way most consumers understand their counterfeit consumption (or rejection of counterfeit consumption) in terms of their attempts to construct how they see themselves, or, indeed, how they want to be seen by others. Several interviewees, including those who had previously bought counterfeit and suggested that they would consider it again in the future (Oliver and Ruby), actually held quite negative perceptions about counterfeits in terms of their views about how wearing a counterfeit might reflect badly upon themselves. This seemed largely to do with the way these respondents perceived counterfeit wearers in a social context and the negative connotations that they felt it would have on their own sense of style and identity. This seemed particularly related to the social groups counterfeits seemed to be associated with such as 'chavs' (see Hayward and Yar 2006 for a discussion regarding 'chavs'), but also could be related back to the discussion of early writers on consumption who focus on class differentiation (such as Leibenstein 1950; Veblen [1899] 1998; and Simmel [1904] 1957). Ruby suggested that she would probably stay away from most counterfeits now because her peers (who could all afford authentic branded goods) might judge her. Ruby also suggested that "I've now started associating fakes with being chavvy". She went on to explain that this was partly because of the association between 'chavs' and Burberry (see Bothwell 2005), and the location of buying counterfeit goods in the UK as being primarily on markets. Thomas (26 years old, full time employed in administrative support role with a low average spend on fashion products) also described one of his experiences when he had come across some counterfeit sportswear:

> I came across some Adidas two stripes, but I wouldn't buy them because of chavs. (Thomas)

Although not explicitly describing 'chavs', Amelia (21 years old, part time student with an average spend of £200–£300 a month on apparel/accessories) and Joshua also related their concerns about wearing counterfeits down to the way they perceive others who do:

> Subconsciously I am going to look at people, so if I saw someone wearing a fake then I wouldn't necessarily not want to speak to them, but I'd make some sort of judgement about them in my head which is a very bad thing to do. (Joshua)

> I wouldn't be seen dead in a fake … and I know unfortunately I'd put a judgement on a person if they are wearing fakes. (Amelia)

Oliver described how certain brands are important to him and how this relates to his views about counterfeits and the perceptions what counterfeits have about his own style:

Oliver: I think my perceptions have changed, once over I was probably all for being able to buy fakes but there are certain brands that you are loyal too that you may feel a little disgruntled if you see a fake. For instance, I'm very into Vivienne Westwood as a designer and I like to have Vivienne Westwood things and that is something I would

	never consider buying a fake of because it wouldn't have the same appeal and I know there are a lot of fakes around and I find that more crippling as I think it takes the edge of mine
Interviewer:	Would it put you off the brand if people were buying a lot of fake Vivienne Westwood?
Oliver:	It probably would yeah. Looking around [Town Name] it was sort of a niche brand and that's why I liked it. But looking around town now I see a lot of the girls who have got the earrings in, although I don't wear earrings I like the accessories and I know that they are probably not real and it's that perception of them becoming a bit common or people perceiving that mine might not be real.

Oliver continued:

> I've probably learnt now to keep away from them, because of the disappointment there is, and they almost don't have that bit of magic about them and you feel bit of a fake yourself wearing them. It takes the edge of them. (Oliver)

Existing research on counterfeiting has considered consumption of counterfeits in relation to self-image scores. De Matos et al. (2007) and Nia and Zaichkowsky (2000) both found that those who do not buy counterfeits see those who do as having a lower image. Bloch et al. (1993: 35) found that those who bought counterfeits saw themselves as having a lower self-image seeing 'themselves as less well off financially, less successful and less confident than other consumers'. However, the discussions above indicate support for viewing counterfeit consumers (or certain types of) as having a lower image, there is little evidence to support that counterfeit consumers see themselves in this way. For some interviewees, negative views about counterfeits was related to the idea of achieving and that by buying the authentic product you have shown that you have been successful. This could be in terms of rewards for savings:

> I'm just a snob ... I've been brought up that if you want something badly you save up and get it.   (Freya)

Or, rewards for working hard:

My money is so important now and I think that if you really work really hard and buy yourself a bag then you pride yourself if you save up but if you didn't you'd know how it feels, but if I don't know I just wouldn't feel happy about it.   (Lily)

THE 'FEEL GOOD' NATURE OF SHOPPING: THE EMOTIVE ASPECTS OF CONSUMPTION

For many consumers although there might be a range of factors which influence what they wanted to buy or wear, they would only actually go ahead and buy it if it "looked good on". This was described very much in terms of how it made them "feel good". This is symbolic of Entwistle's description of how 'wearing the right clothes and looking our best, we feel at ease with our bodies' (Entwistle 2000: 7) If this perception of 'looking good' was reinforced by someone else the desire that "I have to have it" appeared even more difficult to fight. Even in the case when a consumer knew that they could not afford to have the item. As Amelia described:

> I went into Topshop the other day, and I've got no money but in Topshop I saw these lush high waisted shorts and they were like £30, but I had to have them. I was in the changing room and this woman was like 'they look so nice on you'. I had to have them.   (Amelia)

In a hyper-individualised competitive consumer environment which is filled with anxieties and insecurity about how we look the emotional attachment to fashion items and how things can make us feel better appears to be more important than whether we can afford it (see Hall et al. 2008). Amelia went on to describe other situations where the desire to have something was more important than whether she could afford it:

Amelia: I went into Jane Norman and I bought a couple of things in the sale ... I do look at the new stuff, but I will usually go for what is in the sale. Same with River Island, they were having an end of season sale, so I bought a coat.
Interviewer: Why did you buy that coat?
Amelia: Because it fitted me, the fabric was really pretty ... I had to be careful how much I spent that day because I had to lie to my parents about how much I'm spending. But I did buy this really nice top that I didn't expect to buy because it wasn't my style at all, but I liked it. I tried it on and really liked it.

Although many consumers described how browsing for fashion items – online or physically was a pleasurable way to spend their leisure time, actually purchasing something for some, was even more enjoyable. Isabella (22 year old fashion and design student) talked about how she "likes buying" clothes. Ruby described how buying fashion is a "treat":

> I usually just buy things impulsively, if I like it and it's not too expensive …
> I buy clothes just as like a treat.   (Ruby)

Megan (22 year old, fashion and design student) describes how satisfying buying can be:

> But when you do buy something when you've been looking for it there's enjoyment in the satisfaction of seeking out what you've got and buying it.
> (Megan)

Emily (27 years old, full time postgraduate student) also describes how buying can be related to boredom – shopping was an activity seen by several consumers as something to do in your spare time.

> The last time I wanted some clothes and I was bored and I spent a lot. I wanted some new things and to have fun and to treat myself. It was instant gratification.   (Emily)

This idea of "instant gratification" reinforces the importance of how consuming can make you feel. Although many scholars discuss the purpose of fashion as one being that of a communicator (see Veblen [1899] 1998; Liebenstein 1950; Dubois and Duquesne 1993; Baudrillard [1970] 1998) there also is the recognition that consumption is something which is 'fundamentally expected' with consumers having an 'unapologetic, unrepentant sense of desire' (Hayward 2004: 161). Buying clothes and other fashion items can make you 'feel good'. The emotional nature of fashion is something which certainly became apparent through the discussions earlier about peoples' decisions to buy fashion goods. This in a sense then does not mean that emotion should be seen as a polar opposite to rationality. The emotional nature of fashion consumption often takes place within what seems like quite rational consumption in the sense of personal style and identity and not just within impulsive (boredom) purchases such as those described by Emily above. As Yar (2009) argues we should not see emotions as contrary to rationality. Emotions 'can in fact be seen as reasonable (and hence rational) subjective responses' (Yar 2009: 2).

> Sometimes I can see what I 'need' – although I don't really 'need' it at all – I might have an idea, might have seen it on TV, or need to complete an outfit, but sometimes I just buy stuff off the peg. Fit is becoming more something I'm aware of and also how long it will last, I'm moving away from disposable items.   (Emily)

Therefore, in this sense, consumption, although couched heavily in emotions, is entirely rational given the society these consumers live in (Bauman 2007, 2008; Hall et al. 2008; Hall 2012; Smith and Raymen 2018), reflecting the 'cultural injunction to enjoy' (Zizek 2002). However, this moment (or anticipation of the moment) of the feeling good from consuming tends to be short-lived: 'consumption is founded on *lack* – a desire always for something not there ... consumers, therefore, will never be satisfied' (Bocock 1993: 69).

COPYING AND IMITATION: THE BEATING HEART OF FASHION

So far it has been explored why it is necessary to understand the consumption of counterfeit fashion items within the context of consuming fashion. The focus up until this point has been to explore the dynamics of consumer behaviour in relation to fashion and counterfeits with a focus on the product, situation and context of consumption. In developing an understanding of consumption of counterfeit fashion, this position needs to be expanded further to consider how the 'problem' of counterfeiting 'partly lies in the industry itself' (Hilton et al. 2004: 345). This is partly due to concerns about the harmful nature of the legitimate fashion industry as discussed in Chap. 4, but also on a broader conceptual level of the very nature of fashion and its perpetuation of consumer desire, emphasis on false needs, and incredible ability to create a sense of *lack* in consumers to be continually wanting the next thing.

Fashion and the fashion industry, rely on a process of 'introduction and imitation' (Yurchisin and Johnson 2010: 3): a process which is at the heart of stabilising capitalist global economies increasingly reliant on the consumption of products and leisure (Hoskins 2014). This is summarised aptly by the UK's former Minister of State for Universities, Science,

Research and innovation, Jo Johnson in his foreword for the 2016/17 Intellectual Property Crime and Enforcement report

> Commerce is about copying. Making exact, reliable copies of consumer products characterises industrial production. In the creative economy, copying through printing has driven innovation. In digital Britain copying can be instantaneous, faultless and universally available. Guaranteeing the validity of copies is central to the success of all businesses and economies. Today, a 'genuine article' is a 'legitimate copy', protected and identified by intellectual property rights and licences (see IPCG 2017: 4).

Combine with this the very premise of fashion as based on desire. Further, the emphasis within the fashion cycle on *copying* in itself adds to the potential to blur the boundaries between products which are deemed as problematic i.e. counterfeit, and those that are not. The nature of the fashion 'cycle' is one which relies on designs being replicated to the mass market. Designers show their designs on the catwalk (runway) and styles, trends and designs become modified for the mass market and this is distributed to the consumer through fashion magazines, celebrities, advertising, online and in shops (Barnard 2007; Crewe 2017). Therefore, legitimate fashion goods are readily available on the high street with designs closely based on what has been shown on the catwalk at varying price points to attract the consumer to spend money. Part of the role of fashion magazines, vloggers and social media accounts is to perpetuate this – for example features that include advice on how to recreate a particular look seen on celebrities or elsewhere. In essence, fashion relies on imitation for mass production – copying in this sense is accepted because it both publicises the fashion brand, and 'legitimates their designs as ones which are desirable and worth copying' (Hilton et al. 2004: 351).

Copying is also legitimised by fashion brands themselves through ready to wear lines and franchising. This is most aptly demonstrated by the latest trend of brands to 'faux fake' their own products – for example luxury brand Gucci released designs based on 1980s counterfeit products (see Cochrane 2017; Satenstein 2017). At the same time, there is also the visible growth in value retailing and its 'disposable' fashion (shops such as Primark, H&M and Matalan that sell fashion goods at a low price point) and the popularity of 'fast fashion'. This essentially advocates purchasing cheaper items which are often much less durable to enable consumers to keep up with rapidly changing fashion trends. The advent of fast fashion and its resultant speeding up of the fashion cycle (goods can go from pro-duction to consumption within a matter of days), coupled with ever expanding modes and ease of consumption, generates a resounding suc-cess platform for impulse buying. Thus, as well as encouraging consumers to buy cheap products, this can blur the boundaries between counterfeits and non-counterfeits. Discounting of goods, selling of factory rejects, and, parallel trading, all further compound complex discussions around ethics, the fashion industry, and counterfeiting (Hilton et al. 2004). 'The international mass consumer now wants the latest fashion post-haste, necessitating flexibility and turnaround at levels that disrupt all stable norms of industrial competition' (Ross 1997: 11) which will have inevi-table harm attached: counterfeit products or otherwise. Consumption, fundamentally, normalises harm (Hall 2012; Smith 2014; Hall and Winlow 2015; Smith and Raymen 2018).

Chapter Conclusion

Consuming fashion is inherently caught up in both everyday practices of consumption and the emotional desire to 'feel good' – a desire contempo-rary consumer capitalism tells us is fixable through wearing the right clothes, or having the latest look. In attempts to understand the consump-tion of counterfeit fashion it is clear that although factors related to the product and the context of its purchase (such as point of sale, cost, fit) might be important, as are consumer interpretations about what is fash-ionable, what looks good *on them*, explanations which over-emphasise individual choice are problematic. Counterfeit consumption cannot be understood without taking into consideration the consumption of fashion and the nature of the fashion industry. This chapter draws on the position that the nature and sustainability of illegal, or counterfeit, markets is inher-ently situated in the legal market. The demand for counterfeit fashion is established, promoted and reinforced by the 'legitimate' industry.

A continually evolving fashion industry, with daily updates of new 'must have's' (and of course by default the resulting effect of existing goods diminished to *must nots*) provides one of the most effective ways to engage with consumption. For Bauman (2007) this 'buy it, enjoy it, chuck it out cycle' (p. 98) coupled with the 'constant pressure to be *someone else*' (p. 100) reinforces the constant demand in neo-liberal capitalist societies for the consumption of fashion. As Lloyd (2013: 152) summarises:

the genius of consumer capitalism reveals itself in the fact that these desires do not present themselves to us as desire, rather we are convinced that we *need* each specific consumer product. Creating *pseudo-needs* and then ensuring we can never satisfy them ensures the economy keeps going on the back of our thwarted desire.

Although consumers are sold ideals of free choice and identity expression through fashion, the reality is that the nature of fashion is one which is structurally and systemically harmful. Recent critical perspectives on leisure turn our attention to the 'cool individualism' (Hall 2012), that prioritises 'consumer taste and desires as a form of 'freedom' and liberal self-expression' (Smith and Raymen 2018: 67). The ever increasing pressure to consume perpetuated by the cycle of introduction and imitation combines with desire for immediate and emotional gratification. This takes place amongst a social and economic backdrop that, for the majority, is characterised with precarity, anxiety and insecurity (Hall et al. 2008; Lloyd 2013), not to mention an ever increasing consumer debt market (Horsley 2015). The very nature of contemporary fashion serves to exacerbate consumer anxieties in a way which goes far beyond buying clothing items with the inevitable focus it places on the body (Entwistle 2000). Increasingly intertwined with fashion is the unregulated and all-encompassing 'health' and 'wellness' industry. Here we see advocates of quick fix diets, pyramid selling schemes not to mention the self-proclaimed 'lifestyle coaches' and unqualified nutritional advisors. This exists alongside an ever growing beauty and cosmetics industry that enables consumers to manipulate their bodies into the latest fashionable craze. This has moved well beyond make-up products to a range of semi-permanent and permanent body 'fixes': and the inevitable opportunities for harm and illicit markets (see Hall 2019).

In conclusion, understanding the nature of fashion is necessary for a critical debate about fashion counterfeiting. This is largely due to the nature of the fashion process – one of 'introduction and imitation' which is 'repeated over and over again' (Yurchisin and Johnson 2010: 3). Thus, the very nature of fashion and the sustainability of consumer industries are inherently based on copying, but further, embedded in harm (Hall 2012; Smith and Raymen 2018). As Hilton et al. (2004) argue; the very nature of the fashion industry and fashion 'cycle' encourages copying and imitation, and therefore on the one hand conceptually at least would seem to legitimise counterfeiting. However, despite copying and imitation being at the heart of the fashion industry, at some point (for some at least), copying becomes illegitimate and problematic. Intellectual property laws, therefore, exist with a view to protect the 'legitimate' industry from illegitimate copying. The point in which copying becomes counterfeiting, and/or design piracy, although in the one sense guided by law, is also subject to debate. The arguments against counterfeiting which position it as unacceptable copying however largely rests on the notion of 'harm'. This is essential to consider further in seeking to understand the consumption of counterfeit fashion. This point will be examined further in Chap. 4.

REFERENCES

Archer, L., Hollingworth, S., & Halsall, A. (2007). 'University's Not for Me – I'm a Nike Person: Urban, Working-Class Young People's Negotiations of 'Style''. Identity and Educational Engagement. *Sociology, 41*(2), 219–237.

Barnard, M. (2007). Introduction. In M. Barnard (Ed.), *Fashion Theory: A Reader*. Oxon: Routledge.

Baudrillard, J. ([1970] 1998). *The Consumer Society. Myths and Structures*. London: Sage.

Bauman, Z. (2007). *Consuming Life*. Cambridge: Polity.

Bauman, Z. (2008). *Does Ethics Have a Chance in a World of Consumers?* Harvard: Harvard University Press.

Beer, D. (2017). The Social Power of Algorithms. *Information, Communication and Society, 20*(1), 1–13.

Belk, R. W. (1995). Studies in the New Consumer Behaviour. In D. Miller (Ed.), *Acknowledging Consumption: A Review of the New Studies*. London: Routledge.

Bloch, P. H., Bush, R. F., & Campbell, L. (1993). "Consumer Accomplices" in Product Counterfeiting: A Demand Side Investigation. *The Journal of Consumer Marketing, 10*(4), 27–36.

Bocock, R. (1993). *Consumption*. London: Routledge.

Bothwell, C. (2005). Burberry Versus the Chavs. *BBC News Online*. Available from: http://news.bbc.co.uk/1/hi/business/4381140.stm. Accessed 04 May 2011.

Cochrane, L. (2017, December 30). It's a Rip Off: Now Bootleg Logos Are a Fashion Must Have. *The Guardian*. Available from: https://www.theguardian.com/fashion/2017/dec/30/bootleg-logos-designers-copyright-fashion. Accessed 30 Dec 2017.

Crewe, L. (2017). *The Geographies of Fashion. Consumption, Space and Value*. London: Bloomsbury.

De Matos, C. A., Ituassu, C. T., & Rossi, C. A. V. (2007). Consumer Attitudes Towards Counterfeits: A Review and Extension. *Journal of Consumer Marketing, 24*(1), 36–47.

Dubois, B., & Duquesne, P. (1993). The Market for Luxury Goods: Income Versus Culture. *European Journal of Marketing, 27*(1), 35–44.

Elliott, R., & Leonard, C. (2004). Peer Pressure and Poverty: Exploring Fashion Brands and Consumption Symbolism among Children of the 'British Poor'. *Journal of Consumer Behaviour, 3*(4), 347–359.

Entwistle, J. (2000). *The Fashioned Body. Fashion, Dress and Modern Social Theory.* Cambridge: Polity Press.

Grogan, S. (2008). *Body Image. Understanding Body Dissatisfaction in Men, Women and Children* (2nd ed.). London: Routledge.

Guardian. (2018, July 27). Love Island Stars to Cash in on Fame as Series Comes to a Close. *Guardian Online.* Available from: https://www.theguardian.com/tv-and-radio/2018/jul/27/love-island-stars-fame-series-close-itv. Accessed 30 July 2018.

Hall, S. (2012). *Theorizing Crime and Deviance. A New Perspective.* London: Sage.

Hall, A. (2019). Lifestyle Drugs and Late Capitalism: A Topography of Harm. In O. Smith & T. Raymen (Eds.), *Deviant Leisure: Contemporary Perspectives on Leisure and Harm.* London: Palgrave Macmillan.

Hall, S., & Winlow, S. (2015). *Revitalizing Criminology Theory: Towards a New Ultra Realism.* London: Routledge.

Hall, S., Winlow, S., & Ancrum, C. (2008). *Criminal Identities and Consumer Culture. Crime, Exclusion and the New Culture of Narcissism.* Devon: Willan.

Hayward, K. J. (2004). *City Limits: Crime, Consumer Culture and the Urban Experience.* London: The Glasshouse Press.

Hayward, K., & Yar, M. (2006). The Chav Phenomenon: Consumption, Media and the Construction of a New Underclass. *Crime, Media and Culture, 2*(1), 9–28.

Hesse-Biber, S. (1996). *Am I Thin Enough Yet?* Oxford: Oxford University Press.

Hilton, B., Choi, C. J., & Chen, S. (2004). The Ethics of Counterfeiting in the Fashion Industry: Quality, Credence and Profit Issues. *Journal of Business Ethics, 55,* 345–354.

Horsley, M. (2015). *The Dark Side of Prosperity.* Farnham: Ashgate.

Hoskins, T. E. (2014). *Stitched Up. The Anti-Capitalist Book of Fashion.* London: Pluto.

IPCG. (2017). *IP Crime and Enforcement Report 2016–17.* Intellectual Property Crime Group. UK Intellectual Property Office. Newport. Available from: https://www.gov.uk/government/publications/annual-ip-crime-and-enforcement-report-2016-to-2017. Accessed 01 Dec 2017.

Klein, N. (2000). *No Logo.* London: Harper Perennial.

Leibenstein, H. (1950). Bandwagon, Snob and Veblen Effects in the Theory of Consumer Demand. *The Quarterly Journal of Economics, 64*(2), 183–207.

Lloyd, A. (2013). *Labour Markets and Identity on the Post-Industrial Assembly Line*. Basingstoke: Ashgate.

Nia, A., & Zaichkowsky, J. L. (2000). Do Counterfeits Devalue the Ownership of Luxury Brands? *The Journal of Product and Brand Management, 9*(7), 485.

Ritzer, G. (2014). Automating Prosumption. The Decline of the Prosumer and the Rise of the Prosuming Machines. *Journal of Consumer Culture, 15*(3), 407–424.

Rojek, C. (2017). Counterfeit Commerce: Relations of Production, Distribution and Exchange. *Cultural Sociology, 11*(1), 28–43.

Rook, D. (1987). The Buying Impulse. *Journal of Consumer Research, 14*, 189–199.

Rook, D. W., & Gardner, M. (1993). In the Mood: Impulse Buying's Affective Antecedents. *Research in Consumer Behaviour, 6*, 1–28.

Ross, A. (1997). Introduction. In A. Ross (Ed.), *No Sweat. Fashion, Free Trade and the Rights of Garment Workers*. London: Verso.

Satenstein, L. (2017, June 6). Would You Ever Buy Fake Designer Clothes? How Some Labels Are Changing the Bootleg Stigma. *Vogue*. Available from: https://www.vogue.com/article/rise-of-bootleg-fashion-at-gucci-and-vetements. Accessed 30 Dec 2017.

Shaw, J. (2010). *Shopping. Social and Cultural Perspectives*. Cambridge: Polity.

Simmel, G. ([1904] 1957). Fashion. *American Journal of Sociology, 62*(May), 541–558.

Smith, O. (2014). *Contemporary Adulthood and the Night Time Economy*. London: Palgrave.

Smith, O., & Raymen, T. (2018). Deviant Leisure: A Criminological Perspective. *Theoretical Criminology, 22*(1), 63–82.

Solomon, M. R., & Rabolt, N. J. (2004). *Consumer Behaviour in Fashion*. New Jersey: Prentice Hall.

Sweetman, P. (2001). Shop Window Dummies? Fashion, the Body, and Emergent Socialites. In J. Entwistle & E. Wilson (Eds.), *Body Dressing. Dress Body Culture*. Oxford: Berg.

Veblen, T. ([1899]1998). *The Theory of the Leisure Class*. New York: Prometheus Books.

Yar, M. (2009). Neither Scylla Nor Charybdis: Transcending the Criminological Dualism Between Rationality and the Emotions. *Internet Journal of Criminology*.

Yurchisin, J., & Johnson, K. K. P. (2010). *Fashion and the Consumer*. Oxford: Berg.

Zizek, S. (2002). *Welcome to the Desert of the Real*. London: Verso.

CHAPTER 4

The Counterfeit Fashion Industry and Consumer Understandings of Harm

Abstract This chapter explores why consumers buy counterfeit goods within broader discussions around attitudes towards crime, harm and victimisation. In addition to examining the impacts of the counterfeit industry, this chapter examines the inter-related nature of the counterfeit and legitimate industry. Despite debates about counterfeit goods tending to centre on harm (or lack of harm in some cases), it is clear that ideals of direct and deserving victimisation play an important role in shaping responses towards the debate. Despite the notional focus on harm, these debates fail to engage with a consideration of harm that moves beyond the focus on individual consumers, business and criminal activity. The chapter argues that counterfeit consumption needs to be understood within the context of the harmful nature of contemporary consumer capitalism.

Keywords Harm • Attitudes towards crime and harm • Victimisation • Fashion industry

INTRODUCTION

If you buy counterfeit goods, you're helping the trader to break the law. The money you've spent ends up funding organised crime such as drug dealing. You're also contributing to job losses because genuine manufacturers are

© The Author(s) 2019
J. Large, *The Consumption of Counterfeit Fashion*, Palgrave Studies
in Risk, Crime and Society,
https://doi.org/10.1007/978-3-030-01331-8_4

unable to match prices charged by rogue traders. Worst of all, you're putting yourself at risk: some counterfeits can be dangerous to use and in some cases are made using toxic substances. (Action Fraud 2017)

Given the nature of the supply and demand relationship, when it comes to counterfeit fashion goods it is hardly unsurprising that the consumer, is considered fundamental to the transaction. Part of the existing explanation or rationale, for why people consume counterfeit fashion goods is that they do not recognise the harm that counterfeits cause. Therefore, alongside traditional enforcement activities, a consumer responsibility initiative has developed. This approach attempts to educate consumers about the 'dangers' of buying counterfeit goods and is based on idea that if consumers are educated about the harmful nature of counterfeiting, they will cease to purchase (at least in terms of knowingly purchase) counterfeits. This 'awareness raising' also encourages consumers to take more care in where they buy products from: with the aim of reducing the risk of consumers unknowingly purchasing counterfeit products. Hence, one of the primary strategies to reduce supply is to reduce consumer demand. This is most explicitly evident in the UK governments Intellectual Property Enforcement Strategy 2020 (IPO 2016), where one of the three strategic priorities is to 'ensure that' 'consumers and users are educated to the benefits of respecting IP rights, and do so' (IPO 2016: 1). This forms part of a longer term concern about consumer behaviour and attitudes towards counterfeit goods, for example the 2007 Intellectual Property Crime Report suggested that although national strategies against counterfeiting were starting to reap positive outcomes 'the biggest hurdle to overcome is to educate the general public' (IPCG 2007: 5).

This kind of approach assumes that consumers do not recognise the harms of counterfeiting, consider it a 'victimless crime', or, do not take these concerns 'seriously'. Therefore, this chapter aims to explore this assumption further. This chapter first outlines the most common arguments given against counterfeiting in relation to harm and explores consumer attitudes towards harm, crime and victimisation. In addition to examining the impacts of the counterfeit industry, this chapter also examines the inter-related nature of the counterfeit and legitimate industry from a harm based perspective. This in particular highlights consumer concerns about the 'legitimate' fashion industry, and, questions the distinction between legitimate and illegitimate markets. Finally, this chapter will return to the consumer responsibility and education policy agenda, and, consider whether attempts to change consumer behaviour are likely to be successful. Here the chapter will reflect on consumer 'negotiations' of harm. The chapter problematizes criminological explanations that might explain the consumption of counterfeits in terms of resistance, and/ or rejection of social norms and values. Instead, I draw upon advances in critical criminology and zemiology that combine an understanding of the political and economic climate and an understanding of the harmful nature of contemporary consumer capitalism.

The Harmful Nature of Counterfeit Fashion

Industry has, for a number of years, complained that counterfeiting is detrimental to legitimate manufacturers and retailers. This is primarily financial; through 'lost sales' and brand reputation damage. Potential harm to individual consumers also causes concern and provides more of a rationale for 'public' enforcement resourcing. However, the tendency here is to consider 'safety critical counterfeits' as the most problematic (see Yar 2005). Goods typically described as 'non-safety critical' – such as fashion counterfeit products – are suggested to pose less pressing public interest and safety concerns (see Wall and Large 2010). Against, this context, where the focus is solely on the (lack of) harm to the individual consumer (or indeed fashion companies), it is argued that market for counterfeit fashion products is perceived as a 'victimless crime' (Anderson 1999; Patent Office 2004:s4). As discussed in Chap. 1, in these kinds of considerations about harm, conceptions of deception and quality levels are considered important.

Anti-counterfeiting campaigning work in recent years, coupled with national and international intellectual property strategies, has sought to highlight that counterfeiting has harms felt beyond the consumer and trade mark owner. The initial 'Economic Impact of Counterfeiting' report produced by the OECD two decades ago, provided at the time, the most comprehensive examination of the 'costs' of counterfeiting, suggesting that harm is evident in four main ways (OECD 1998). Firstly are the 'costs to the rights holder' (i.e. the owner of the legitimate trademark that is being counterfeited). Secondly, the economic and social costs to the countries where counterfeiting production happens. Thirdly, are the 'costs to the countries were counterfeits are sold', and finally the fourth type of costs are reported to be the various 'social costs' of counterfeiting that includes. Since the 1998 report, a number of other national and internationally focused publications have continued to outline the harms of counterfeiting (often in the terminology of 'impacts') and emphasise its relationship with serious and organised crime (see for example OECD/ EUIPO 2016; IPO 2016; IPCG 2017; May 2017). Although there are inevitable variations in legislation and policy across Europe and the rest of the world that shape differing responses and strategic priorities, one consistent message remains clear: counterfeiting is harmful and the 'fake goods industry is not the victimless crime you might imagine it to be' (Europol 2017).

Returning to the UK's current IP enforcement strategy, the following statement is made about the problem of counterfeiting and IP crime:

> ...strong links between IP crime and benefit fraud, organised crime, drug dealing and violence – and this has a real impact on the safety of individuals and communities. Criminal trade also drives out legitimate traders, leading to reduced levels of investment and prosperity in local areas and reduced opportunities for local employment. Other types of harm caused by IP crime include:
>
> * Harm to consumers – directly through dangerous goods, and indirectly through the consequences of sub-standard products;
> * Disruption of community wellbeing by the domination of criminal activity;
> * Economic harm to rights-holders and allied industries supporting legitimate trade, plus unfair competition to legal traders and loss of revenue to Government in terms of tax and duty payments;
> * The involvement of serious and organised crime that benefits from substantial profits; and
> * The use of IP crime to fundraise for terrorist activity (IPO 2016: 15)

There is an implication that consumers are naïve, and are unaware of these harms and crimes, and, that through education their behaviour can be changed. Some organisations are vocally critical of consumers, suggesting that even when they do recognise financial, economic or social harms they dismiss them, or do not take them seriously (AIM 2005). In 2005, the AIM Briefing Paper (p4) argued that the 'proof' that counterfeiting is not taken seriously can be seen in

> the tourist who blithely refuses to accept that his purchase of a cheap T-Shirt helps to sustain a serious and organised criminal culture that may also be directly linked with funding international terrorist groups.

The language of the IP Crime and Enforcement Report 2016/17 (IPCG 2017: 8) that suggests 're-educating consumers is a key priority' [emphasis added], appears to support this assumption. Therefore, this chapter next moves onto examining consumer perspectives in relation to fashion counterfeiting, crime and harm.

CONSUMER PERSPECTIVES ON COUNTERFEITING, CRIME & HARM

The manufacture, production, and, retailing of counterfeit goods, is in most jurisdictions an offence under criminal law. However, what tends to receive most emphasis from law enforcement and regulatory agencies is the suggestion that counterfeiting activities are potentially high profit and, therefore, are attractive to organised criminal groups and networks. In addition, this concern extends to the likelihood that those involved in counterfeiting are likely to be involved in criminal activities such as 'money laundering, people trafficking, loan sharking and the exploitation of children' (IPCG 2010: 15). Most anti-counterfeiting literature focuses on the general problem of counterfeiting, although there are examples of fashion counterfeiting specifically as an activity linked to organised crime and also terrorism. The AAIPT Report (AACP undated: 14) cites the Threat Assessment Report 2002 (Northern Ireland Organised Crime Task Force) that 'confirms that 34% of the organised crime groups in Northern Ireland were involved in product counterfeiting' (including clothing). The Threat Assessment Report further claims that counterfeit goods to the value of £6.7 million were seized in 2002. This leads the AAIPT to conclude that:

> The scale of these offences means not only that they are, by definition, the work of organised criminal groups, but also – given the nature of criminality in the Province – it is inconceivable that terrorist organisations are not directly complicit (AACP undated: 14).

There certainly appeared to be a concern from consumers that these kinds of claims against counterfeiting were exaggerated or misleading, and although for some consumers this meant that they dismissed such claims, for others they recognised some form of truth within them. A number of consumers, in the qualitative section of the exploratory survey and the interviews, saw the potential for counterfeiting to have a relationship with wider criminality.

My main concern with fake fashion goods are exploitation of cheap labour and the profits funding criminal activity, i.e. money laundering, illegal drugs, terrorism etc. (26 year old female, non-counterfeit buyer)

Yes there is a link with organised crime, forcing people into labour, intimidation and violence. There is also problems of tax evasion and then harms to legitimate companies. There are also ethical trading issues – sources etc. (Emily, 27 year old female, had previously bought a counterfeit but would not do so again)

Anything unlawful like that is probably going to be fuelling something more horrendous, that's probably the wrong word. Those are massive reasons that make it worse than a company losing money, it's much worse than that. (Chloe, 24 year old female, had previously bought a counterfeit but would not do so again)

Yes the people who counterfeit are likely to be the same people who do piracy [pirate] videos. That thing that happened with the Chinese people, the illegal immigrants that died [cockle pickers] and they found out that the people who bought them into the country were illegally counterfeiting, selling drugs... (Amelia, 21 year old female, had never previously bought a counterfeit and would not consider doing so)

For some consumers, although they recognised that counterfeiting might well be associated with harmful activities, they were not so convinced of links to 'serious' and 'organised' crime.

Yeah I think there is a link, but I don't know what, but I get a feeling. These people are most likely to be shop lifting on mass and probably drugs as well, but then I don't think that is that serious. I don't really disbelieve the links to serious and organised crime but I'm not really sure. (Evie, 27 year old female, had never previously bought a counterfeit and would not consider doing so)

Evie's comments highlight an issue that is recognised by those such as the IPCG. A survey conducted by the IP Office asked authorities involved in counterfeiting enforcement to provide intelligence on whether counterfeiting was linked to 'wider criminality'. The IPCG's report found that there was a range of links with 'lower level' types of criminal and anti-social behaviour, with benefit fraud being the most common at 48 percent

(IPCG 2010: 16). The IPO in 2016, gathered evidence from local authority Trading Standards teams, suggesting that counterfeiting was linked to benefit fraud, drug dealing and violence, in addition to money laundering and organised crime groups (IPO 2016: 15).

The debate surrounding counterfeiting's financing role in organised crime and as a source of income for terrorist activity, is both contested and contentious (see also Antonopoulos et al. 2018). Terms like organised crime and terrorism are often used un-problematically and interchangeably in many anti-counterfeiting policy discussions. Further, the notion of organised crime is one that tends to be used as a blanket way of describing counterfeiting and related criminal activities. For example, the National Crime Agency in the United Kingdom, who cite counterfeiting as 'attractive' to 'organised criminals', defines organised crime as

> serious crime planned, coordinated and conducted by people working together on a continuing basis. Their motivation is often, but not always, financial gain. Organised criminals working together for a particular criminal activity or activities are called an organised crime group (National Crime Agency 2017).

Although critiques of the use of the term organised crime are well versed in criminology (see Hobbs 1998, 2002, 2013; Levi 2007, 2014; Croall 2010; von Lampe 2016 for discussions), expecting the public to have any real understanding of organised crime and what constitutes it or how it works are likely ambitious. Further, there may be a number of (potentially valid) reasons why consumers do not believe claims surrounding counterfeiting or think they are exaggerated. Asking consumers explicitly about fashion counterfeiting as a crime problem tended to be met with some form of ambivalence or confusion. Although this appears to provide evidence for the need for awareness raising campaigns, in terms of ambitions to change consumer behaviour, it should be noted that attitudes may not equate to realities of consumer behaviour.

> Buying fake fashion goods is a small crime compared to burglary etc. (20 year old male, non-counterfeit buyer)

> To be honest with the levels of real crime (drugs, prostitution etc) in Britain I couldn't give a tiny rat's arse about fake goods! Sorry to be rude but that's my true opinion! (18 year old female, non-counterfeit buyer)

> I don't think it's that big of a problem, I think there are worse things out there than that. (Mia, 24 year old, had never bought a counterfeit and did not intend to do so in the future)

Much of the discussions around crime with consumers tended to reflect subjective notions of seriousness or 'real' crime (Box 1983). This is reflective of concerns by those such as Brookman et al. (2010: 85) who note how 'social attitudes' towards crimes such as counterfeiting 'are often quite different' to more 'traditional crimes' (see also Rojek 2017). Consumers' views about the 'seriousness' of crime seemed largely attributable to where they perceived direct victimisation to lay: this was often caught up in discussions around the brand ideas of 'ideal', 'deserving' or 'undeserving' victimisation (see for example Christie 1986). Although a number of consumers did consider counterfeiting in terms of criminality in some way – for some it was theft or stealing, others it was more about what the proceeds of counterfeiting could be used to fund – it tended to be considered as 'less serious' than other forms of crime. Here, distinctions about types of counterfeiting seemed to be important – for example some consumers who were willing to buy counterfeit fashion, would not be prepared to buy counterfeits they considered to be harmful to themselves such as medicines – and further, just because a consumer would not buy counterfeits, did not mean that they would not engage in other forms of intellectual property crime. Joshua, for example, discussed how he would not buy counterfeit fashion, but does regularly download music illegally. In terms of allocations of public policing resourcing, how consumers appeared to understand and construct notions of crime had implications on how they felt resources should be spent.

The Harmful Nature of the (Counterfeit) Fashion Industry

Despite claims that consumers do not recognise the harms of counterfeiting, a very different picture emerges from consumers once getting beyond superficial statements. Although language tended to steer away from terms such as 'crime', many consumers described concerns about exploitation of workers and poor working conditions.

> Over the past couple of years I've become aware that when fashion goods are cheap there is likely to be an element of exploitation in their production – I think I'm less bothered about tax revenue or authenticity of brands

and more concerned about the conditions of workers who produce the goods. I know that lots of high street brands are guilty of exploiting workers in developing countries – my main concern with fake fashion items would be that working conditions could be even less regulated and more exploitative. (29 year old female, knowing counterfeit buyer)

Issues of worker exploitation, and especially child labour exploitation, do tend to be cited in counterfeiting policy discourse, as are moral arguments about the need to protect designers and trade mark owners. Although there might be some attribution of victim status for those involved in production stages of the counterfeit supply chain, the tendency is to consider counterfeiting as simply a problematic activity.

The majority of counterfeit items come from factories in the Far East, 'staffed' by children who are paid very little, have no labour rights and work up to 18 hours a day (Europol 2017).

Given that the argument against counterfeiting is so heavily engrained in concerns about harm, exploitation and crime, it is interesting that in any official discourse, there is never any kind of recognition about the potential positive impacts of a counterfeit industry, nor, how counterfeiting might impact on different places or social groups in different ways: some of which may be beneficial. The assumption is that it is always bad. Although this is a provocative suggestion, if concerns about counterfeiting are couched in notions of harm, morals and ethics, there should at least be an examination of the potential positive impacts of counterfeiting. Hilton et al. (2004) have argued that moral arguments could be used to actually justify the acceptance of counterfeiting:

Given that many operate in countries where they face economic hardship, some might consider it a basic human right to make a living whatever way one can in order to survive (Hilton et al. 2004: 349).

Some consumers framed their concerns about workers within discussions of poverty and limited opportunities to employment. Selling counterfeits, or working for factories that might produce counterfeit goods, was considered by some, a better employment alternative than other options.

I suppose that I do live in the naïve bubble I think well they're just making a bit of money for themselves it's their business and they're supporting their family and that's the way they are doing it. A market stall over there is just like a market stall over here. I think everyone is genuine, they might be selling counterfeits but it's just their way of making money for their family. (Erin, 46 year old, had previously bought counterfeits)

I'd rather them doing that [people making counterfeits] than like something worse on the streets doing drugs and god knows what. (Poppy, 19 years old, had previously bought counterfeits)

I don't think I am particularly concerned about it, I think child labour goes on either way... Where I used to work, they found it in our factories and there was nothing they could do about it because it was a legal document that the children had to sign to say they were over age. So there is a lot of things that go on... Yeah, like one girl was like 12 and she bought a piece of paper for 50 rupees from the town hall saying that she was 30 with 3 children, and they can't dispute it because it's a legal document. It doesn't influence my decision to buy things because they used to be prostitutes, so they have only gone from prostitution to working in a factory. So it's a little bit better. (Amy, 22 years old, previously had bought counterfeits)

Consumer rationalisations demonstrate how as consumers, we negate and justify concerns we hold about how our consumption habits harm. This is often done through a process of othering, reflecting cultural judgements popular amongst consumers from the Global North (see Mostafanezhad 2017). However, rather than providing a solution to convincing consumers not to buy counterfeit fashion, highlighting the potential victimisation of counterfeit trading, surely questions the need for a more critical discussion around illicit and licit global consumer industry? Should we instead be challenging the acceptance of harm as a normal aspect of consumption (see Smith 2014; Smith and Raymen 2018)?

Concerns About Legitimate Fashion Companies

Many consumers who described concerns about the ethical issues of manufacturing and producing counterfeits, also reflected on concerns with the manufacture and production of fashion goods more generally. Although fashion companies would be inclined to deny any poor procedure, there has been evidence of poor practice in the past (see Ross 1997; Branigan 1999; Klein 2005; Dickson 2005; Panorama 2008; Hoskins 2014; Brooks 2015) and consumers certainly seem to be under the belief that this is still taking place. Although an obvious response by the fashion companies might be that this does not matter as it is not true, in terms of developing a more critical understanding of counterfeiting this is very relevant. Particularly because anti-counterfeiting strategies may find difficulty in persuading consumers not to buy counterfeit products on the grounds of worker exploitation and poor production practices if consumers believe that this is happening in the legitimate fashion industry anyway (see Large 2015).

> I've never thought of counterfeiting interestingly as contributing any more than any other industry to like sweat shop labour. It's something I think unless things hugely change, will always exist. It's a real slow process where change might happen. The fact that it's linked to organised crime means that it must be difficult to legislate for counterfeit products as opposed to other products where there is a clear chain to legislate on, so I suppose that's raising an issue to me, now I'm thinking about it that could mean that harm is caused by the industry. I've always thought of all consumer industries as potentially damaging. (Ella, 27 years old, has not previously bought a counterfeit but might consider doing so in the future)

> Well one I was thinking about were the ethical practices of production like buying a pair of shoes with a Nike stripe on for £100 that they've paid some 12 year old girl in Indonesia to make for 50pence. I think there's a repugnant side to labels and branding. I think if I was confident a brand had very ethical practices then that might change things but I think there is a lot of moral bankruptcy in the whole idea of brands and branding. (Alfie, 38 years old, has bought counterfeits previously and would again)

Some consumers had a very specific idea about those fashion brands that had poor ethical practices. Primark was frequently mentioned as problematic:

> Primark was the worst, so it does make me think but I don't actually think about it with fake fashion, I don't know. I would never buy Nike, I don't like the idea of big companies. Primark, I'm on the edge with although I do like the cheap clothes and I do think to myself [about ethical concerns] and I only occasionally buy from there. There are some brands I wouldn't buy from. (Olivia, 27 years old, had previously bought counterfeits)

> Yeah, if you think it's sort of a similar realm of things like the Primark thing – illegal immigrants working in really bad conditions, I kind of think

there could be something related yeah, like the idea of children doing these bags. I think it must be illegal somewhere along those lines. (Lily, 24 years old, had previously bought counterfeits but would not do so again)

There is a tendency to point the blame finger at value retailers whose business model is based on high volume sales of cheap, disposable items such as Primark – especially as a result of the Panorama documentary aired in 2008 (Panorama 2008), that highlighted issues such as child labour and poor production practices. However, these issues are not exclusive to value retailers (Siegle 2011; Hoskins 2014; Brooks 2015). Poor production practices are commonly associated with unsafe working conditions. For instance, the collapse of the Rana Plaza, a factory in Savar, Bangladesh in April 2013 produced new calls for scrutiny on the global fashion industry. More than 1000 factory workers were killed and over 2000 more injured in a factory that collapsed only a day after it was ordered to be closed due to safety concerns (Hoskins 2014; Jones 2016; Scott 2018). Rana Plaza housed a number of popular global high street fashion brands, a number of whom appear yet to take financial responsibility towards compensating victims' families (see Clean Clothes Campaign 2017a). In July 2016, 38 people were formally charged with murder following the collapse (Guardian 2016) – although it is not clear at the time of writing to what extent this case has progressed. However, this was not a one off incident, only a few months prior to the Rana Plaza collapse was the Tazreen Fashions Factory fire, again in Bangladesh that killed 112 workers and injured scores of others. This fire was one of a number of clothing factory fires in the years preceding (Human Rights Watch 2015). Consumers, as do those such as Hoskins (2014) and Brooks (2015), also question whether problems of this nature just lay with value retailers (see also Lloyd 2019 for a wider discussion around labour markets and harm). Evie for example suggested: "Primark is really bad for ethics but I don't think Topshop is much better". The comments of Olivia and Alfie above both also pinpointed Nike as problematic. For some consumers, the fact that Primark is a value retailer means that their poor practices are less problematic than those of other companies that generally charge much more for their fashion products.

No because I think that's all in the fashion industry even I think in a way Armani whoever are possibly worse because they are possibly getting them nearly as cheaply as Primark, but at least Primark are honest, they say they get cheap labour and they sell the clothes cheap. I'm sure Armani don't pay much more than Primark to kids and abuse them, but are making a massive more profit for themselves. (Erin)

When that documentary came on about Primark like, it kind of made me think 'awww' but at the same time I thought they are selling their products so much cheaper so you expect, so you subconsciously kind of think something is dodgy, but if Levi, Armani or Gucci were doing the same thing, the mark up on their T-Shirts is just ridiculous, it's obviously like 100% profit. That's what make me think I don't want to spend my money with you [expensive brands] because at the end of the day I'd rather they get paid and for me to go out and buy cheaper products. (Poppy)

These high profile events brought global scrutiny on the global fashion industry and generated questions about the working standards, conditions and safety of the workers employed to produce these fashion goods and a succession of contract stipulations from brands and national laws to formally address concerns. However the success of legislation and regulation is questionable (see Tombs 2004; Tombs and Whyte 2007). Human Rights Watch (2015) reported:

consistent violations of worker's rights in factories including practices contrary to both national law and codes of conduct Western retailers insist suppliers use.

The report based on research with workers from numerous factories across Bangladesh, found violations that included: physical abuse, sexual abuse, verbal abuse, forced overtime, failure to pay wages on time or in full, dirty drinking water and pressure to not use the bathroom (Human Rights Watch 2015). Despite a recognition that unions are one of the most effective ways to make a workplace safer (Tombs 2004) Human Rights Watch further found that attempts to set up unions often result in dismissals, pay refusal and assault. December 2016 witnessed mass dismissals of workers in factories supplying global brands such as H&M, Gap and Zara for protesting about low pay (Safi 2016; Clean Clothes Campaign 2017b). In addition, concerns remain about the exploitation of children. Quattri and Watkins (2016: 3) report that there is a 'high work incidence of children aged 6–14' years old; children who are working 'beyond just a few hours a day'. Although Quattri & Watkins' report focused on child labour in Bangladesh generally, in terms of the fashion industry, it was found that the garment sector accounts for two thirds of female child labour. Children, therefore, are exposed to the same dangers as adult workers in these environments, but are even more vulnerable due to their age. Most children who are working are not in education (Quattri and Watkins 2016). Work by Lloyd (2019) and Scott (2018) explores in more depth the wider range of social harms experienced by workers. These kinds of social harms are imperative to consider in recognition of their overwhelming exacerbation of social inequalities and impact on the economically disadvantaged (Yar 2012; Hall and Winlow 2015; Pemberton 2015).

In addition to the concerns about workers, the relationship between the fashion industry and environmental harm is one that warrants further attention. EcoWatch (2015) suggests that the fashion industry is 'the second dirtiest industry in the world' after oil. Ho and Choi (2012) note the 'negative ecological footprint' that the industry leaves behind – primarily due to high volume, low value manufacturing and the complexity and speed of the supply chain. There are two issues of environmental concern here. First the waste, pollution and impact generated from manufacturing and supply – including production processes, transportation and energy consumption – that is evident at all stages of the supply chain. Environmental concerns include the carbon footprint, depletion of water resources and the amount of waste from the production processes (see WRAP 2017). However, also of relevance is waste post-consumption, that as Hvass (2014) argues, is a growing problem compounded by the growth of value retailing and fast fashion (Morgan and Birtwistle 2009; see also Brooks 2015). In the UK alone in 2005, DEFRA (2007) estimated that 2 million tonnes of textile waste is generated every year, with more than half of that ending up in landfill. Attempts to reduce clothes ending up in landfill through recycling and reuse have witnessed a reduction in the amount sent to landfill since 2012, yet the consumption of fashion items remains on the increase (WRAP 2017). Additionally, reuse and recycling schemes are themselves not free from harm (see Brooks 2015 for a critical account of the second hand clothing industry).

Some consumers are changing their buying habits, for example both Daisy and Emily stated that because they were becoming increasingly aware of the damaging nature of disposable fashion to the environment, they were becoming less concerned about price, and now were prepared to pay more money for better quality items that would last longer. Harrison et al. (2005: 2) describe this type of consumption as 'ethical purchase behaviour' or 'ethical consumption' where price and quality are still important factors, but additionally so are concerns about ethics. This ethical concern is not only applied to environment, but for some consumers such as Evie and Ella it also affected their decisions where to shop (or avoid). Issues of harmful waste disposal practices, whether legal or illegal, tend to affect the poorest in the world the most (White and Heckenberg 2014). The tendency for wealthy countries to export their waste to less developed countries is well documented, as is the tendency for waste disposal sites in communities to be located in the most disadvantaged areas (see White and Heckenberg 2014). However, 'ethical consumption' is itself questioned as little more than a marketing ploy justifying more expensive products with a 'feel good' factor (see Brisman and South 2014 and Brooks 2015 for good discussions). As Smith and Raymen (2018) argue ethical consumption is not a 'conscious awakening of an ethical heart of capitalism'. Ethical schemes can be seen instead as part of the.

> overwhelming tendency to look at individualistic rather than systemic harms that has allowed these supposedly benevolent capitalists to disavow the much deeper systemic harms of a global capitalist system to which they are vital contributors (Smith and Raymen 2018: 76).

These issues are not just the problem of low value and high street fashion brands. As Hoskins (2014) argues, there is little value in separating 'high' fashion and 'high-street' fashion in any examination of the global fashion industry. This is because luxury fashion houses rely on mass-production of items such as T-Shirts, bags and sunglasses for profits in similar locations and manners to high-street or 'fast fashion' brands. Further, on a wider conceptual level as Hoskins asks, 'why pretend over-consumption is a problem of only the cheapest brands?' (2014: 3). Bringing us back to the work of critical criminologists, and in particular, ultra-realists (see Hall and Winlow 2015), Jack recognises that the problems might lie with the models of fashion consumption:

> I think the brands are very unethical. Possibly, Nike shirts produced for instance if we look at things like corporation and the workers and the working discretion, you know the industry out there does it have the guts to claim that there are ethical issues? I think that there might be, but no more than there are some issues we already have especially in some fashion – Zara's and the Primark's and also the legal models. We also have to buy cheap and then dispose of it in a few months. (Jack, 32 years old had previously bought counterfeits although at the time thought they were genuine).

Although the discussion around harm has shifted focus to the legitimate fashion industry, these issues are relevant to the shadow counterfeit industry. Thus on the one hand although it is clear that attention needs to be afforded to the harms of the fashion industry, the harms of the counterfeit industry are likely to be exacerbated by the lack of any kind of scrutiny or regulation. Therefore, it is evident that if we move beyond binary definitions and a view of harm that is largely constructed in terms of crime and illegality, there is a need to examine closely the harms of the legitimate and illegitimate fashion industry. It is also evident, that the fashion industry is at least partly responsible for the shadow counterfeit fashion industry. Ray Hudon's work on the need to move beyond distinctions between legal and illegal is useful in recognising not only the problem of this kind of distinction, but the temporal, spatial and cultural nature of how we define legality, morality and acceptability (Hudson 2019) and reflects the need for criminologists to be more attuned to the harms of consumer industries (see Smith and Raymen 2018).

Reducing the Demand for Counterfeit Fashion

Most consumers do recognise that fashion counterfeits have ethical issues related to their manufacture and production; this is true for those who do and do not knowingly buy counterfeit goods. Additionally, although not everyone considers fashion counterfeiting as a priority crime problem, or necessarily believes the relationship counterfeiting is said to have with other forms of criminal activities there is a general recognition on some level of counterfeiting both as a crime, and as a trade that is harmful. However, although this may be the case, there is a contested viewpoint about the extent to that consumers' feel *they* should be concerned about this, or change their behaviour because of it. Two points appear to be important. The first is that consumers may negate their concerns about the harms of counterfeiting because they see the legitimate fashion industry as being guilty of similar practices and problems. The second is that despite suggestions that counterfeiting is considered a 'victimless crime' and that explains why consumers are willing to not take responsibility for counterfeiting, consumers *do* recognise issues that could be characterised as harmful. They just do not necessarily describe counterfeiting of fashion goods in terms such as crime or harm. This appears to be partly associated with their understanding (or lack of understanding) about what constitutes crime and harm, and further, notions around seriousness and victimisation. Asking consumers directly using a survey style methodology may well appear to indicate that consumers see counterfeiting as a 'victimless crime', yet more qualitative discussions exploring their views appears to question this presumption.

However, what is clear is despite a consumer's choice of terminology, or how much of a problem they consider counterfeiting, the majority of counterfeit consumers do see it in some way as *bad*. However, just because something is recognised as harmful – does it mean that people won't continue to do it? This is a problematic assumption to make given many consumers' views on the legitimate industry. Psychological research on behavioural intentions, such as that of Ji and Wood (2007), tends to suggest that people will often continue to follow their existing consumption 'habits' even when they might have intended to do otherwise.

> Sometimes when I see something that has a lot of detail on it, I'll think 'aww that poor person must have taken ages doing that'. I do sometimes think that but I don't think I'm not going to buy it now. I would still buy it anyway. Don't I sound really selfish? (Poppy)

> I used to actively avoid ethically bad shops and I don't shop at Gap because of the child labour issues... Primark had a big backlash so it enacted an ethical policy and a load of stores said they reinvented policy, but as soon as the media went away it then went back to child labour. But I don't know what the alternative is apart from expensive fair trade boring bland products. (Evie, 27, post graduate student, never knowingly bought counterfeit)

> I suppose like some of it is like slavery and that, a lot of clothes are made on the back streets of India and in the slums. So you have got all of that, that I do know about because I saw it on TV. But I wouldn't say that it bothers me too much because that's just how it is. It's just how it is isn't it? (Charlie, male, 29, labourer, previously unknowingly bought counterfeits)

Thus, it appears clear that consumers do recognise some of the problems associated with counterfeiting when these are understood in an understanding of harm. Whether it is something they feel they should be concerned about is contestable. For some consumers, recognition of harm was one of the primary reasons they would not consume counterfeits. For others, although they recognised counterfeits as harmful, the extent this might change their behaviour was less clear.

> If I actively bought fakes then maybe [change my mind about buying fakes] but because I've only rarely bought fakes like being on holiday, and when you're on holiday you forget a bit about your morals and things like that, but in an everyday situation if I came across a market and I knew it was funding child labour, I suppose I think to myself, because Primark is one organisation you can say that it is associated, but with fakes it's loads of different people, you could only say generally fakes are associated with poor labour conditions etc., so that almost escapes you of your responsibility because you could justify yourself by saying that fakes may be generally but they're not. (Olivia)

Olivia's comments here reflect notions of Presdee's (2000) 'moral holiday', but also complement suggestions from Chap. 2 that when people are on holiday they might act differently to how they would otherwise. However, there are inherent contradictions within consumer viewpoints. The idea that consumers can be educated to not buy counterfeits based on making them aware of related harm ignores the issue that many consumers buy legitimate items from an industry they recognise as harmful. This problematizes the idea that educating consumers about the harms of counterfeiting is an effective solution to the counterfeit industry (Large 2015). Olivia, above, talks explicitly about the notion of self – responsibility and importantly, being able to escape it because essentially there is not one clear victim. Thus, although recognising what she is doing is in some way harmful, justifies her behaviour anyway – as we can also see in the comments of Charlie, Evie and Poppy earlier.

Throughout the research with consumers, 'techniques of neutralisation' appeared evident (Sykes and Matza 1957). *Denial of responsibility* appeared through either saying that they did not realise they were buying a counterfeit at the time, further refusal to take personal responsibility with a general sense of counterfeits being a legitimate means of engaging in fashion. The *denial of injury*, as was *denial of the victim* was evident in many of the discussions about harm and crime. This was closely related to *condemnation of the condemners* – where the perceived poor processes of the fashion industry legitimised counterfeiting. In fact, through condemning the fashion industry this appeared to neutralise any harm that consumers did recognise. As touched upon briefly, counterfeit consumption although appearing to be less about peer group behaviour and more about allegiance to style, fashion and identity preferences that can broadly be interpreted as *appeal to higher loyalties*. However, although this could be suggested that it helps us understand how consumers negotiate their behaviour in relation to the actual act of buying a counterfeit, it fails to help us understand people's consumption of fashion. This appears to be the point we need to move towards, since essentially, engaging with *illicit* goods, is an extension of engaging with *licit* goods – which consumers do recognise as harmful. To understand the demand for illicit markets, we need to move beyond focusing only on the illicit market and provide a more critical understanding of the parallel legal market. This should involve recognising the harms that are associated with the legal market and the overlapping relationship between the licit and illicit – particularly within the context of a globalised consumer market (Hudson 2019). Here it appears more useful to draw on the work of Bauman (2008: 52–53) who argues that in a globalised consumer society

> the concepts of responsibility and responsible choice, that used to reside in the semantic field of ethical duty and moral concern for the Other, have moved or have been shifted to the realm of self-fulfilment and calculation of risks.[...] 'Responsibility' means now, first and last, *responsibility to oneself* ('you owe this to yourself').

The idea of educating consumers about harm to get them to take responsibility is therefore a problematic intention. This will be discussed more fully in the final chapter, where it is argued that due to the inherently harmful nature of global consumer capitalism, we need to move away from an abject focus on individual responsibility, morals and ethics.

CONCLUSION

This chapter has explored the counterfeit fashion industry in relation to discussions around crime and harm. This chapter first outlined the most common arguments against counterfeiting in relation to crime and harm before exploring how this relates to consumer views. This focused on exploring the seeming disconnection between on the one hand the serious criminality and harm counterfeiting is said to promote and on the other hand, the suggestion that fashion counterfeiting is largely considered a victimless crime (Anderson 1999; Patent Office 2004:s4). Insight into consumer attitudes is useful here as changing consumer behaviour is considered a key strategic priority for enforcement. This approach is based on an assumption that consumers do not recognise the harms of counterfeiting, and if they are 'educated' about these, then they will cease to purchase counterfeits. This reduction in demand will help reduce the supply of counterfeit goods. This chapter explored the problems with these kinds of attempts.

Despite debates about counterfeit goods tending to centre on harm (or lack of harm in some cases), it is clear that ideals of direct and deserving victimisation play an important role in shaping responses towards the debate. Thus, despite the notional focus on harm, it can be argued that these debates fail to engage with a thorough and critical consideration of social harm that moves properly beyond the focus on individual consumers, legitimate business and largescale criminal activity. This chapter problematizes examining counterfeiting within a framework constrained by 'crime' though expanding the argument that it is problematic to consider the illicit market of counterfeits alone. A framework based on conceptions of crime and criminal law constrains notions of harm and victimisation and fails to critically consider the harms that are perpetuated by the legitimate industry (Tombs 2004, 2010; Tombs and Whyte 2007; Hall and Winlow 2015; Smith and Raymen 2018).

REFERENCES

AACP. (undated). *Proving the Connection. Links between Intellectual Property Theft and Organised Crime*. Alliance Against Intellectual Property Theft (formerly Alliance Against Counterfeiting and Piracy). Available from: http://www.allianceagainstiptheft.co.uk/downloads/reports/Proving-the-Connection.pdf. Accessed 10 Sept 2007.

Action Fraud. (2017). Counterfeit Goods Fraud. Action Fraud National Fraud and Cyber Crime Reporting Centre. Available from: https://www.actionfraud.police.uk/fraud_protection/counterfeit_goods. Accessed 1 Dec 2017.

AIM. (2005, April). *Faking It: Why Counterfeiting Matters*. Briefing Paper. Association des Industries de Marque. European Brands Association. Brussels

Anderson, J. (1999). The Campaign Against Dangerous Counterfeit Goods. In R. E. Kendall (Ed.), *International Criminal Police Review: Special Issue on Counterfeiting*. Lyon. ICPO/Interpol. Available from: http://counterfeiting.unicri.it/docs/International%20Criminal%20Police%20Review.pdf. Accessed 13 June 2011.

Antonopoulos, G. A., Hall, A., Large, J., Shen, A., Crang, M., & Andrews, M. (2018). *Fake Goods, Real Money. The Counterfeiting Business and Its Financial Management*. Bristol: Policy Press.

Bauman, Z. (2008). *Does Ethics Have a Chance in a World of Consumers?* Harvard: Harvard University Press.

Box, S. (1983). *Power, Crime and Mystification*. London: Routledge.

Branigan, W. (1999, January 14). Top Clothing Retailers Labelled Labour Abusers: Sweatshops Allegedly Run on US Territory. *The Washington Post*.

Brisman, A., & South, N. (2014). *Green Cultural Criminology: Constructions of Environmental Harm, Consumerism and Resistance to Ecocide*. London: Routledge.

Brookman, F., Maguire, M., Pierpoint, H., & Bennett, T. (2010). Part Two: Fraud and Fakes – Introduction. In F. Brookman, M. Maguire, H. Pierpoint, & T. Bennett (Eds.), *Handbook on Crime*. Devon: Willan.

Brooks, A. (2015). *Clothing Poverty. The Hidden World of Fast Fashion and Second-Hand Clothes*. London: Zed.

Christie, N. (1986). The Ideal Victim. In E. A. Fattah (Ed.), *From Crime Policy to Victim Policy*. Basingstoke: Macmillan.

Clean Clothes Campaign. (2017a). *Rana Plaza*. Available from: https://clean-clothes.org/safety/ranaplaza. Accessed 6 Jan 2017.

Clean Clothes Campaign. (2017b). *Press Release 05.01.17: Bangladeshi Garment Workers Face Mass Firings and Criminal Charges*. Available from: https://cleanclothes.org/news/2017/01/05/bangladeshi-garment-workers-face-mass-firings-and-criminal-charges. Accessed 6 Jan 2017.

Croall, H. (2010). Middle-Range Business Crime. In F. Brookman, M. Maguire, H. Pierpoint, & T. Bennett (Eds.), *The Handbook on Crime*. Devon: Willan.

DEFRA. (2007). *Maximising Reuse and Recycling of UK Clothing and Textiles*. London: Department for Environmental Food and Rural Affairs.

Dickson, M. A. (2005). Identifying and Profiling Apparel Label Users. In R. Harrison, T. Newholm, & D. Shaw (Eds.), *The Ethical Consumer*. London: Sage.

EcoWatch. (2015). *Fast Fashion Is the Second Dirtiest Industry in the World, Next to Big Oil*. EcoWatch. Available from: http://www.ecowatch.com/fast-fash-ion-is-the-second-dirtiest-industry-in-the-world-next-to-big%2D%2D188208 3445.html. Accessed 6 Jan 2017.

Europol. (2017). *Counterfeit Products: Why Buying Fakes Can be Bad for Your Health (and more)*. Europol. The Hague. Available from: https://www.europol.europa.eu/publications-documents/counterfeit-products-why-buy-ing-fakes-can-be-bad-for-your-health-and-more. Accessed 1 Dec 2017.

Guardian. (2016). Rana Plaza collapse: 38 Charged With Murder Over Garment Factory Disasters. *The Guardian*. Available from: https://www.theguardian.com/world/2016/jul/18/rana-plaza-collapse-murder-charges-garment-fac-tory. Accessed 6 Jan 2017.

Hall, S., & Winlow, S. (2015). *Revitalizing Criminological Theory. Towards a New Ultra –Realism*. London: Routledge.

Harrison, R., Newholme, T., & Shaw, D. (2005). Introduction. In R. Harrison, T. Newholm, & D. Shaw (Eds.), *The Ethical Consumer*. London: Sage.

Hilton, B., Choi, C. J., & Chen, S. (2004). The Ethics of Counterfeiting in the Fashion Industry: Quality, Credence and Profit Issues. *Journal of Business Ethics, 55*, 345–354.

Ho, H. P. Y., & Choi, T. M. (2012). A Five-R Analysis for Sustainable Fashion Supply Chain Management in Hong Kong: A Case Analysis. *Journal of Fashion Marketing and Management, 16*(2), 161–175.

Hobbs, D. (1998). Going Down the Glocal. The Local Context of Organised Crime. *The Howard Journal of Crime and Justice, 37*(4), 407–422.

Hobbs, D. (2002). The Firm: Organisational Logic and Criminal Culture on Shifting Terrain. *British Journal of Criminology, 42*(1), 549–560.

Hobbs, D. (2013). *Lush Life. Constructing Organised Crime in the UK*. Oxford: Oxford University Press.

Hoskins, T. E. (2014). *Stitched Up. The Anti-Capitalist Book of Fashion*. London: Pluto.

Hudson, R. (2019). Economic Geographies of the (il)legal and the (il)licit. In T. Hall & V. Scalia (Eds.), *A Research Agenda in Global Crime*. London: Edward Elgar.

Human Rights Watch. (2015). *Whoever Raises Their Head Suffers the Most. Workers' Rights in Bangladesh's Garment Factories*. Available from: https://www.hrw.org/report/2015/04/22/whoever-raises-their-head-suffers-most/workers-rights-bangladeshs-garment. Accessed 6 Jan 2017.

Hvass, K. K. (2014). Post-Retail Responsibility of Garments – A Fashion Industry Perspective. *Journal of Fashion Marketing and Management, 18*(4), 413–430.

IPCG. (2007). Intellectual Property *Crime Report*. Intellectual Property Crime Group. UK Intellectual Property Office. Available from: http://www.ipo.gov.uk/ipcreport07.pdf. Accessed 10 Feb 2008.

IPCG. (2010). Intellectual Property *Crime Report 2009–2010*. Intellectual Property Crime Group. UK Intellectual Property Office. Available from: http://www.ipo.gov.uk/ipcreport09.pdf. Accessed 15 Aug 2011.

IPCG. (2017). IP Crime and Enforcement Report 2016–17. Intellectual Property Crime Group. UK Intellectual Property Office. Newport. Available from: https://www.gov.uk/government/publications/annual-ip-crime-and-enforcement-report-2016-to-2017. Accessed 1 Dec 2017.

IPO. (2016). Protecting Creativity, Supporting Innovation: IP Enforcement 2020. Intellectual Property Office. Newport. Available from: https://www.gov.uk/government/uploads/system/uploads/attachment_data/file/571604/IP_Enforcement_Strategy.pdf. Accessed 16 Dec 2017.

Ji, M. F., & Wood, W. (2007). Purchase and Consumption Habits: Not Necessarily What You Intend. *Journal of Consumer Psychology, 17*(4), 261–276.

Jones, R. (2016). *Violent Borders. Refugees and the Right to Move*. London: Verso.

Klein, N. (2005). *No Logo*. New York: Harper.

Large, J. (2015). Get Real Don't Buy Fakes. Fashion Fakes and Flawed Policy: The Problem with Taking a Consumer – Responsibility Approach to Reducing the Problem of Counterfeiting. *Criminology and Criminal Justice, 15*(2), 169–185.

Levi, M. (2007). Organised Crime and Terrorism. In M. Maguire, R. Morgan, & R. Reiner (Eds.), *The Oxford Handbook of Criminology* (4th ed.). Oxford: Oxford University Press.

Levi, M. (2014). Thinking About Organised Crime. *The RUSI Journal, 159*(1), 6–14.

Lloyd, A. (2019). *The Harms of Work. An Ultra-Realist Account of the Service Economy.* Bristol: Policy Press.

May, C. (2017). *Transnational Crime and the Developing World.* Washington DC: Global Financial Integrity [GFI].

Morgan, L. R., & Birtwistle, G. (2009). An Investigation of Young Fashion Consumers' Disposable Habits. *International Journal of Consumer Studies, 33,* 190–198.

Mostafanezhad, M. (2017). *Volunteer Tourism. Popular Humanitarianism in Neoliberal Times.* London: Routledge.

National Crime Agency. (2017). Crime Threats. Available from: http://www.nationalcrimeagency.gov.uk/crime-threats/intellectual-property-crime. Accessed 16 Dec 2017.

OECD. (1998). *The Economic Impact of Counterfeiting.* Organisation for Economic Co-Operation and Development. Available from: http://www.oecd.org/dataoecd/11/11/2090589.pdf. Accessed 27 July 2011.

OECD and EUIPO. (2016). *Global Trade in Fake Goods Worth Nearly Half a Trillion Dollars a Year,* Organisation for Economic Co-Operation and Development [OECD] and European Union Intellectual Property Office [EUIPO]. Available from: http://www.oecd.org/industry/global-trade-in-fake-goods-worth-nearly-half-a-trillion-dollars-a-year.htm. Accessed 22 Oct 2016.

Panorama. (2008, Monday 23rd June). Primark: On the Rack. *Panorama. BBC One.* Available from: http://news.bbc.co.uk/1/hi/programmes/panorama/7461496.stm. Accessed 13 June 2011.

Patent Office [Now Known as the UK Intellectual Property Office]. (2004). *Counter Offensive: An IP Crime Strategy.* Department for Trade and Industry (DTI). Available from: http://www.ipo.gov.uk/ipcrimestrategy.pdf. Accessed 12 June 2011.

Pemberton, S. (2015). Harmful Societies. In *Understanding Social Harm.* Bristol: Policy Press.

Presdee, M. (2000). *Cultural Criminology and the Carnival of Crime.* London: Routledge.

Quattri, M., & Watkins, K. (2016). *Child Labour and Education. A Survey of Slum Settlements in Dhaka*. Overseas Development Institute. London. Available from: https://www.odi.org/sites/odi.org.uk/files/resource-documents/11145.pdf. Accessed 06 Jan 2017.

Ross, A. (Ed.). (1997). *No Sweat. Fashion, Free Trade and the Rights of Garment Workers*. London: Verso.

Rojek, C. (2017). Counterfeit Commerce; Relations of Production, Distribution and Exchange. *Cultural Sociology, 11*(1), 28–43.

Safi, M. (2016). Bangladesh garment factories sack hundreds after pay protests. *The Guardian*. Available from: https://www.theguardian.com/world/2016/dec/27/bangladesh-garment-factories-sack-hundreds-after-pay-protests. Accessed 6 Jan 2017.

Scott, S. (2018). *Labour Exploitation and Work-Based Harm*. Bristol: Policy Press.

Siegle, L. (2011). *To Die for. Is Fashion Wearing Out the World?* London: Harper Collins.

Smith, O. (2014). *Contemporary Adulthood and the Night Time Economy*. London: Palgrave.

Smith, O., & Raymen, T. (2018). Deviant Leisure: A Criminological Perspective. *Theoretical Criminology, 22*(1), 63–82.

Sykes, G. M., & Matza, D. (1957). Techniques of Neutralisation: A Theory of Delinquency'. *American Sociological Review, 22*(6), 664–670.

Tombs, S. (2004). Workplace Injury and Death: Social Harm and the Illusions of Law. In P. Hillyard, C. Pantazis, S. Tombs, & D. Gordon (Eds.), *Beyond Criminology: Taking Harm Seriously*. London: Pluto.

Tombs, S. (2010). Corporate Violence and Harm. In F. Brookman, M. Maguire, H. Pierpoint, & T. Bennett (Eds.), *Handbook on Crime*. Devon: Willan.

Tombs, S., & Whyte, D. (2007). *Safety Crimes*. Devon: Willan.

von Lampe, K. (2016). *Organised Crime. Analysing Illegal Activities, Criminal Structures & Extra Legal Governance*. London: Sage.

Wall, D. S., & Large, J. (2010). Jailhouse Frocks: Locating the Public Interest in Policing Counterfeit Luxury Fashion Goods. *British Journal of Criminology, 50*(6), 1094–1116.

White, R., & Heckenberg, D. (2014). *Green Criminology. An Introduction to the Study of Environmental Harm*. Oxon: Routledge.

WRAP. (2017, July). *Valuing Our Clothes. The Cost of UK Fashion*. WRAP. Available from: http://www.wrap.org.uk/sites/files/wrap/valuing-our-clothes-the-cost-of-uk-fashion_WRAP.pdf. Accessed 2 Jan 2018.

Yar, M. (2005). A Deadly Faith in Fakes: Trademark Theft and the Global Trade in Counterfeit Automotive Components. *Internet Journal of Criminology*. www.internetjournalofcriminology.com.

Yar, M. (2012). Critical Criminology, Critical Theory and Social Harm. In S. Hall & S. Winlow (Eds.), *New Directions in Criminological Theory*. Oxon: Routledge.

CHAPTER 5

The Consumption of Counterfeit Fashion

Abstract Despite the importance of the consumer in counterfeiting policy, there has been a lack of attention within criminology about the demand for counterfeit goods. A tendency to explain counterfeit consumption through deviance or 'othering'; reinforces stereotypical assumptions about consumers and overplays the importance of superficial factors in consumption. This book seeks to develop a better understanding of why counterfeit markets exist when we know that many consumers knowingly buy counterfeit products and argues there is a need to consider demand for illicit goods within the context of consumer capitalism. Through focusing on the end market consumption of counterfeit fashion; a grey area in terms of criminality, and a topic on the border of more traditional criminological concern this book is concerned with the embedded nature of harm in consumer capitalism.

Keywords Fashion counterfeits • Harm • Nature of consumption • Licit • Illicit markets

THE CONSUMPTION OF COUNTERFEIT FASHION

This book aimed to provide the first critical exploration into the consumption of counterfeit fashion goods by way of addressing the underpinning research question *why do people buy counterfeit fashion goods?* Following setting out the context and background to the counterfeit industry in

© The Author(s) 2019
J. Large, *The Consumption of Counterfeit Fashion*, Palgrave Studies in Risk, Crime and Society,
https://doi.org/10.1007/978-3-030-01331-8_5

Chaps. 1 and 2 provided the initial exploration into the consumption of counterfeit fashion goods through investigating popular ideas about counterfeit consumption and consumers. Although inevitably cost was found to be an important factor in the decision to buy a counterfeit the nature of something being 'cheap' is subjective. Assuming that consumers buy counterfeits 'because they are cheap' is simplistic. Further, the growth of disposable fashion and value retailing suggests that consumers do not necessarily equate something being 'cheap' as poor quality, or undesirable. Importantly, there appears little support for the related idea that counterfeit consumers are typically young and from low income backgrounds. Counterfeit consumption takes place across a broad range of consumers of different ages, backgrounds and occupations. Expenditure on counterfeit fashion can also vary considerably.

The situation and context of counterfeit consumption for some consumers was very important. For example, some consumers described that they would buy counterfeits abroad, but this was not something they would do in the UK. This appeared to be about ease of access and availability of counterfeits in certain destinations and reduced concerns about (il)legality. This was particularly the case when consumers visited countries where genuine items were also produced, or, where counterfeiting was considered so rife it was felt difficult to buy something genuine. On the one hand, for some consumers it was more difficult to recognise the cues that might indicate something is counterfeit and, on the other hand, there appeared to be less of a concern about a goods authenticity. The heightened level of counterfeit consumption, particularly for consumers on holiday, also reflected 'going shopping' as a key leisure practice for tourists. The increase in global travel, and emphasis on travel as a primary leisure activity, may well be a factor in the popularity of counterfeit fashion consumption, particularly for more opportunistic buyers.

The increasingly globalised consumer, and, evolving nature of technology, also reflects shifts in consumption of fashion online. Although initially many consumers appeared reluctant to purchase fashion goods in particular from the internet (unless it was something they were buying from a store they were familiar with), how we consume has shifted dramatically and we now see more ways than ever to consume. The nature of shopping has changed as we now live in an era where we can purchase goods with ease from an app on our mobile phone and consumption is increasingly shaped by automated digital technologies. There are also increasingly blurred lines between the producer (retailer) and consumer with it now easier than ever for consumer-to-consumer selling. In terms of counterfeits, it is increasingly easy for those selling counterfeits to infiltrate legitimate supply chains, and, harder for consumers to recognise counterfeits: existing cues about quality, price or website are often meaningless in these new retail environments. At the same time, it is easier than ever for consumers to seek out counterfeits: automated advertising through algorithms will further ensure this process. In terms of the role of situation and context, the internet can be suggested to play a similar role to being abroad: a greater willingness to engage in what might be considered 'risky' behaviour, and, a further blurring of the boundaries between licit and illicit products and markets.

Daily updates of new 'must have's' (and of course by default the resulting effect of existing goods diminished to must nots) provides one of the most effective ways to engage with consumption. For Bauman (2007) this 'buy it, enjoy it, chuck it out cycle' (p98) coupled with the 'constant pressure to be *someone else*' (p100) reinforces the constant demand in neo-liberal capitalist societies for the consumption of fashion. Chapter 3 examined how consuming fashion is inherently caught up in both everyday practices of consumption and the emotional desire to 'feel good'. In attempts to understand the consumption of counterfeit fashion it is clear that although factors related to the product and the context of its purchase (such as point of sale, cost, fit) might be important, as are consumer interpretations about what is fashionable, what looks good *on them*, explanations that over-emphasise individual choice are problematic. Counterfeit consumption cannot be understood without taking into consideration the consumption of fashion *and* the nature of the fashion industry. Therefore, the nature and sustainability of illegal, or counterfeit, markets is inherently situated in legal consumption. The demand for counterfeit fashion is established, promoted and reinforced by the 'legitimate' industry. This is perpetuated by the very nature of fashion being inherently based on copying. As Hilton et al. (2004) argue; the very nature of the fashion industry and fashion 'cycle' encourages copying and imitation, and therefore on the one hand conceptually at least would seem to legitimise counterfeiting.

However, despite copying and imitation being central to the fashion industry, at some point (for some at least), copying becomes illegitimate and problematic. Intellectual property laws therefore exist with a view to protect the 'legitimate' industry from illegitimate copying. The point in that copying becomes counterfeiting and or design piracy although in the one sense guided by law, is also subject to debate. The arguments against counterfeiting that position it as unacceptable copying however largely rests on the notion of 'harm'. However, as noted by Hudson (2019), boundaries between the licit and illicit, legal and illegal, acceptable and non-acceptable are spatially, temporally and culturally constructed.

Recognising the importance of the notion of harm, Chap. 4 further explored consumer behaviour and the counterfeit fashion industry in relation to discussions around crime and harm. Here the focus was on exploring the seeming disconnection between on the one hand, the serious criminality and harm counterfeiting is said to promote, and on the other hand, the suggestion that fashion counterfeiting is largely perceived as a victimless crime (Anderson 1999; Patent Office 2004; Rojek 2017). Insight into consumer attitudes is useful here as changing consumer behaviour is considered a key strategic priority for enforcement. This approach is based on an assumption that consumers do not recognise the harms of counterfeiting, and if they are 'educated' about these, then they will cease to purchase counterfeits. This reduction in demand will help reduce the supply of counterfeit goods. This chapter explored the problems with these kinds of attempts. Indeed, bigger questions remain about a (selective) national and international policy focus that aims to prevent and reduce harm, and whether this neglects to fully engage with both a broader understanding of social harm and factors generating demand for illicit goods/services within a context of global social and economic inequalities.

The Problem of Demand

The consumer appears frequently in the counterfeiting debate in three broad ways. First the consumer is highlighted in many of the discussions about how we assess and typify counterfeiting and harm. For example, distinctions between goods that are safety critical and non-safety critical have an implicit emphasis on the impact on the end user (consumer) of the product. Discussions around victimisation and harm tend also to highlight the consumer particularly in discussions around quality and deception. The second issues rests with the explicit policy task that seeks to change consumer behaviour in the case of those who knowingly buy counterfeits, but also implicitly for those consumers who do not take proper responsibility in guarding against buying counterfeit goods unintentionally, or for those who do not report counterfeit goods being sold. The third way in that the role of the consumer is visible is the recognition that demand is one of the key drivers for intellectual property crime.

Attention towards the consumer and their responsibility for counterfeiting has taken increasing precedence in regulatory and policy frameworks that seek to address counterfeiting. In its most simple form the basic presumption of this approach is if consumers cease to purchase counterfeits then there will be less demand for the supply of counterfeits. Consumers are told to 'not buy fakes' because they are harmful and it is assumed once they are educated about the harms of counterfeiting they will change their behaviour and stop buying counterfeits. Part of the awareness raising campaign seeks to explicitly target those who knowingly buy counterfeit goods, these consumers are considered especially problematic by some as they are seen as refusing to accept the harmful nature of counterfeiting. Other educational style campaigns focus on getting the broader majority of otherwise 'law abiding' consumers to take responsibility for making sure they do not buy counterfeits unintentionally by suggesting 'top tips' to avoid fakes.

Yet, we remain in a situation where despite increased attention from criminologists towards understanding the *supply* of counterfeit goods, much of what is known about the consumption (or *demand*) of these goods tends to come from industry sources or outside of criminology. As a result, the consumption of counterfeit products tends to be understood as something outside of usual consumer behaviour, with an implication that the practice is deviant, or at least different. This has led to suggestions that the counterfeit consumer can be considered as a 'minority' who can be identified either by their demographic characteristics, their lax moral standards or their rejection of consumer capitalism. These assumptions fundamentally underpin the policy attempts to change consumer behaviour. However, the temporal, spatial and cultural nature of how we define legality, morality and acceptability (Hudson 2019) reflects the need for criminologists to be more attuned to the harms of consumer industries (see Smith and Raymen 2018) and question the emphasis on (lack of) morality and deviance of individuals as something that can be altered within the structures of consumer capitalism (Hall 2012).

Conclusions

Despite the evidential importance of the consumer in the counterfeiting realm there has been a lack of attention within criminology about the demand for counterfeit goods (and counterfeit goods more generally), and there is a wider lack of attention to understanding why people buy counterfeit goods when moving beyond superficial explanations. As explored above, this is problematic, especially for policy attempts to change consumer behaviour, but also for criminological attempts to understand the nature of illicit markets. Through exploring the consumption of counterfeit fashion goods this book sought to address this gap and identifies four main points. First of all, attempts to understand the consumption of counterfeit goods in terms of 'deviant' or 'non-normative' behaviour is problematic. This is because there is a lack of evidence to suggest that counterfeit buyers are demographically different to non-counterfeit consumers. Further, through exploring the attitudes of consumers it is suggested that counterfeit buyers do not have different (or 'other') norms and values to non-counterfeit consumers. Consumer rationalisations demonstrate how concerns we might hold about our harmful consumption habits are justified through 'special liberty' – capitalisms extendable 'leash' (Hall 2012). Counterfeit fashion consumption should therefore not be considered as separate, or in opposition, to fashion consumption and it is more useful to consider it as an extension to existing consumption habits and preferences.

Secondly, I argue that counterfeiting needs to be understood in terms of the context it is taking place in, in terms of an understanding of parallel legitimate industry, but also consumption more generally. This means we should not ignore the wider nature of global consumer capitalism which is based on competitive individualism and hyper consumption (Hall 2012). The very nature of consumer capitalisms economic growth and success is based on a perpetual cycle of consumer insecurities and anxieties situated in *lack;* encouraging consumers to display their individuality, have the latest look, products and experiences. Consumer industries adapt, evolve and mutate to create this continual cycle of desires, needs and instant gratification, all the time perpetuated and shaped by rapidly advancing digital technologies and accompanied by new opportunities for illicit markets, crime and harm (see Hall 2012).

The third point reiterates that focusing on crime and criminal law definitions places fashion counterfeiting at the boundaries, or periphery, of criminology and fails to consider critically the potentially embedded and systemically harmful nature of consumer behaviour that on the surface, seems less problematic than more traditional areas of criminological concern. By placing the emphasis on harm (especially when policy and enforcement strategies emphasise harm as much as crime), a much more thorough examination of issues in relation to victimisation is possible, which does not prioritise human harm over non-human harm (see White 2013) and allows an examination of harms not constrained by preconceived notions of crime and law (see Hillyard et al. 2004; Hall and Winlow 2015; Smith and Raymen 2018). Further, as argued by Smith and Raymen (2018: 66), not only can we move to addressing the broad range of harms related to culturally acceptable behaviours, but we can address 'the willingness of individuals to inflict primary or secondary harms upon others' in their pursuits of leisure and consumption.

On the fourth and final point, it is clear that if policy and enforcement strategies wish to shape or change consumer behaviour, there needs to be greater awareness of the issues with ignoring the illicit activities and harms of the legal market. Further, attempts to convince consumers not to buy copies, when the very nature of fashion is essentially based on copying, will always remain a challenge. The 'moral elasticity' and 'moral ambivalence' (see Rojek 2017) that is quite clearly evident in consumer justifications and explanations of counterfeit consumption, appears to be less of a defining feature when it is combined with consumer justifications and explanations of consuming fashion more generally. Therefore, since we could suggest that 'harm is invisible, embedded within the social organisation of consumer capitalism' (Raymen and Smith 2016: 402), there is a need to go beyond focusing on the *crime* problem (i.e. fashion counterfeits) and consider the broader issue of the corrupt, abusive and harmful nature of the fashion industry. By focusing predominantly on illicit markets there is a lack of examination of the harm caused by the licit market – in this case the fashion industry. This is not to dismiss concerns surrounding the counterfeit market but to argue the need for an approach that recognises the embedded nature of harm in fashion.

Through transcending traditional notions of crime, criminality and the 'criminal other', the examination of counterfeit fashion as a criminological topic demonstrates many of the limitations of mainstream criminological theory at dealing with contemporary global issues that do not fall neatly within traditional constructs and conceptualisations of crime and victimisation. By focusing on the non-criminal aspect of the counterfeit supply-demand transaction, on a topic that on appearance sits outside of the criminological agenda, a critical exploration of harm and crime can be undertaken. As the examination of fashion counterfeits demonstrates, if criminology is to understand illicit markets, we need to move beyond simply focusing on the illicit market as if it exists separately and provide a more critical understanding within the context of the parallel legal market. Here it is useful to draw on Rojek's (2017) description of counterfeiting as a 'parasitic' industry. From a demand perspective, this is partly because consuming illicit goods is an extension of consuming licit goods. Within the example of fashion counterfeiting there are further clear parallels between the legitimate and illegitimate market, and a question of whether the fashion industry should shoulder some of the responsibility for the counterfeit industry. This should involve recognising the harms that are associated with the legal market and the overlapping relationship between the licit and illicit – particularly within the context of a globalised consumer market. Recognising a broad array of harms beyond those defined legally as crime is essential, as is recognising the role of the capitalist economic system (Hillyard and Tombs 2004). Instead of seeing counterfeit consumption as deviant, 'other' or rejecting of social norms, values or power relations, following work on the harms of commodified leisure by Smith and Raymen (2018), it is more helpful to position counterfeit consumption as something that is a 'transgression of the ethical duty to the other' (Bauman 2008). Consuming counterfeit fashion can be interpreted then, not as 'transgressing but conforming to capitalism's disavowed core 'values' and practices, that are exploitative, acquisitive and socially irresponsible' (Hall and Winlow 2015: 51).

REFERENCES

Anderson, J. (1999). The Campaign Against Dangerous Counterfeit Goods. In R. E. Kendall (Ed), *International Criminal Police Review: Special Issue on Counterfeiting*. Lyon: ICPO/Interpol. Available from: http://counterfeiting.unicri.it/docs/International%20Criminal%20Police%20Review.pdf. Accessed 13 June 2011.

Bauman, Z. (2008). *Does Ethics Have a Chance in a World of Consumers?* Harvard: Harvard University Press.

Bauman, Z. (2007). *Consuming Life*. Cambridge: Polity.

Hall, S. (2012). *Theorizing Crime and Deviance. A New Perspective*. London: Sage.

Hall, S., & Winlow, S. (2015). *Revitalizing Criminological Theory. Towards a New Ultra-Realism*. London: Routledge.

Hillyard, P., Pantazis, C., Tombs, S., & Gordon, D. (Eds.). (2004). *Beyond Criminology: Taking Harm Seriously*. London: Pluto.

Hillyard, P., & Tombs, S. (2004). Beyond Criminology. In P. Hillyard, C. Pantazis, S. Tombs, & D. Gordon (Eds.), *Beyond Criminology: Taking Harm Seriously*. London: Pluto.

Hilton, B., Choi, C. J., & Chen, S. (2004). The Ethics of Counterfeiting in the Fashion Industry: Quality, Credence and Profit Issues. *Journal of Business Ethics, 55*, 345–354.

Hudson, R. (2019). Economic Geographies of the (il)legal and the (il)licit. In T. Hall & V. Scalia (Eds.), *A Research Agenda in Global Crime*. London: Edward Elgar.

Patent Office [Now Known as the UK Intellectual Property Office]. (2004). *Counter Offensive: An IP Crime Strategy*. Department for Trade and Industry (DTI). Available from: http://www.ipo.gov.uk/ipcrimestrategy.pdf. Accessed 12 June 2011.

Raymen, T., & Smith, O. (2016). What's Deviance Got to Do with It? Black Friday Sales, Violence and Hyper-Conformity. *British Journal of Criminology, 56*, 389–405.

Rojek, C. (2017). Counterfeit Commerce; Relations of Production, Distribution and Exchange. *Cultural Sociology, 11*(1), 28–43.

Smith, O., & Raymen, T. (2018). Deviant Leisure: A Criminological Perspective. *Theoretical Criminology, 22*(1), 63–82.

White, R. (2013). *Environmental Harm: An Eco-Justice Perspective*. Bristol: Policy Press.

INDEX

© The Author(s) 2019
J. Large, *The Consumption of Counterfeit Fashion*, Palgrave Studies in Risk, Crime and Society,
https://doi.org/10.1007/978-3-030-01331-8

Printed in the United States
By Bookmasters